BECOMING A KNOWLEDGE-SHARING ORGANIZATION

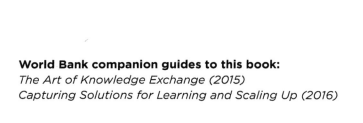

BECOMING A KNOWLEDGE-SHARING ORGANIZATION

A Handbook for Scaling Up Solutions through Knowledge Capturing and Sharing

Steffen Soulejman Janus

CONTENTS

ABOUT THIS HANDBOOK

This volume offers a simple, systematic guide to creating a knowledge-sharing practice in your organization. It shows how to build the enabling environment and develop the skills needed to capture and share knowledge gained from operational experiences to improve performance and scale up successes. Its recommendations are grounded on the insights gained from the past seven years of collaboration between the World Bank and its clients around the world—ministries and national agencies operating in various sectors—that are working to strengthen their operations through robust knowledge sharing.

While this handbook has been informed by the academic literature on knowledge management and organizational learning, its operational background and many real-world examples and tips also provide a practical foundation for public sector officials in developing countries and for development practitioners. Moreover, the overall concepts and approaches will also hold true for most organizations in the private sector and the developed world.

Chapters 1–4 address the enabling environment needed by an organization to systematically identify, capture, and share relevant operational experiences. Chapters 5–8 detail the technical skills required to execute the program. These eight topic areas, or pillars, represent the capacities organizations need, and the actions they can take to develop them. Chapter 9 summarizes the essential points; an extensive appendix includes templates, checklists, a sample knowledge asset, and sample job descriptions. Public sector organizations around the world have found that using the framework presented here has moved them strongly ahead in their quest to capture, use, share, and scale up their experiences and knowledge.

The chapters are in some respects sequential, but they are also modular. Feel free to browse and apply them in any sequence that suits you. The World Bank's two companion guides to this book can take you more deeply into the subjects covered here:

» *The Art of Knowledge Exchange* (2015)

» *Capturing Solutions for Learning and Scaling Up* (2016)

Although this is a handbook, it is not a cookbook. No manual can provide a one-size-fits-all prescription for organizational change or anticipate all the details and issues that will vary across organizations. But we hope that, by offering practical approaches that others have found useful, this guide will help your organization become more effective in systematically capturing and sharing knowledge and taking solutions to scale.

ACKNOWLEDGMENTS

I would like to thank the many colleagues, partners, peers, and friends who have been instrumental in the creation of this book.

First of all, I thank the government of the Republic of Korea and its Ministry of Strategy and Finance for making this publication possible. Korean institutions have long been at the forefront of knowledge sharing for development, and many of the examples of knowledge sharing in this book concern projects that benefited from Korea's cooperation and financing.

I am grateful for my colleagues in the Organizational Knowledge Sharing Program at the World Bank, who have shaped and fine-tuned the approaches and tools described in this handbook through their work with numerous country institutions across the globe. In particular, a big thank-you goes to Jeff Kwaterski and Oscar de Bruyn Kops for their input and guidance on the text, especially in the early stages of drafting.

Abha Joshi-Ghani, Laurent Besançon, and Roby Senderowitsch have provided continuous support and encouragement. It is thanks to them that this book became a reality.

Deep appreciation goes to Gregg Forte for his editorial work in tightening and focusing the manuscript and brightening it with his quick grasp of the value and promise of knowledge sharing.

A special thank you goes to the seasoned knowledge and learning specialists who graciously agreed to review the manuscript: Daan Boom, Manuel Contreras, Maria Gonzalez de Asis, Phil Karp, Vincent Ribiere, and Kelly Widelska. This handbook is the richer for their valuable insights and thoughtful comments.

Finally, as my many hours of work away from home these past few years were the incubator for this book, I will be ever grateful to my loving wife Couro, and to Aisha and Ilias, for the understanding and support they so generously gave me.

Steffen Soulejman Janus
Program Manager,
Organizational Knowledge Sharing Program
Leadership, Learning, and Innovation Vice Presidency,
The World Bank

INTRODUCTION

Many development challenges are common across the world, but the solutions to them usually remain localized—they never get adapted for replication, or the key element is forgotten. Yet some agencies and some localities are more effective at learning from success and applying it further over time and space. What is the difference between those who make progress and those who fall behind?

The answer is as simple as it is complex: *knowledge*—captured knowledge acquired in a specific local context that is adapted, scaled up, and replicated so that fertilizers get to the farmer, children get enrolled in schools, communities are sheltered from natural disasters, and life-saving medicines reach their destination.

Knowledge sharing is the conduit through which solutions travel from place A to place B. But, quite often, rather than being documented and shared, solutions are simply left behind, hidden in remote rural communities or tucked away in the heads of officials and development practitioners who have moved on to the next big task. Knowledge gained from development solutions is permanently at risk of getting lost or forgotten.

Since 2008, the World Bank Group's Organizational Knowledge Sharing Program, initially housed at the World Bank Institute and later at the Vice Presidency for Leadership, Learning, and Innovation, has engaged with country officials and development practitioners on how to systematically take local knowledge to scale: how to capture lessons learned from experience; how to package and store those lessons so that they can be retrieved and shared effectively and so that others—inside the institution and beyond—can benefit from them; and how overstretched and understaffed organizations can deal with "yet another task" called knowledge sharing.

This introductory chapter explores the meaning and importance of being a knowledge-sharing organization. It presents some key concepts and outlines the framework on which the next eight chapters of this handbook are built. And like most of those chapters, it features a snapshot of a specific endeavor ("Knowledge Sharing in Action") that illuminates a productive, real-life engagement with knowledge sharing in the developing world.

Knowledge-Sharing Organizations—What Are They and Why Are They Important?

A knowledge-sharing organization systematically learns from its mistakes and builds on its successes. It sees knowledge as an important currency and values its operational experiences as opportunities for learning for both staff and external partners. Hence, knowledge-sharing

Knowledge Sharing in Action

Knowledge-Sharing Is Helping to Scale Up Solutions for HIV-AIDS Control in India

India's National AIDS Control Organisation (NACO)

In India, HIV/AIDS is an enormous barrier to development, currently costing more than 100,000 lives per year. At the same time, the prevalence of HIV/AIDS in India is declining—the annual number of new cases has fallen by half since 2002. India's National AIDS Control Organisation (NACO), a division of the Ministry of Health and Family Welfare, was launched in 1992 to implement the country's new National AIDS Control Programme. India's response to the epidemic is widely considered to be an instructive model, as is NACO itself.

NACO works closely with 35 official HIV/AIDS societies throughout the country and also engages with nongovernmental organizations and research groups. It faces three tough knowledge-management tasks:

1. Distribute the latest and most relevant knowledge and how-to guidance to its own staff members and partners wherever and whenever needed

2. Preserve institutional knowledge in an environment of staff turnover and the ongoing need to quickly handle mission-critical tasks

3. Manage the increasing domestic and international demand from peer organizations to learn from its experience

NACO realized that it needed a more systematic approach in all these areas:

» Internally—promote collaboration, knowledge capturing, and knowledge sharing across teams and departments to solve complex operational challenges

» Domestically—extend those efforts to its partner organizations, especially across states

» Internationally—strengthen its management of knowledge-sharing requests—which are valuable as an opportunity for both sides to learn and a source of additional partnerships—to take advantage of them without compromising ongoing operations. A major step in that direction was the 2013 creation of the South to South Knowledge Exchange Secretariat

In other words, NACO aims to move from ad hoc responses to complex knowledge demands to becoming a knowledge-sharing organization.

organizations have the potential to continuously improve service delivery—their own and that of peer organizations in their country and throughout the world.

However, knowledge-sharing organizations are not born—they are made. They must decide to overcome natural barriers to knowledge sharing. *Becoming* a knowledge-sharing organization requires leadership that encourages needed changes in culture, provides supportive governance structures and financing, and encourages external partnerships, all to develop the disciplined practice of knowledge capture, learning, and sharing (see box I.1). Those organizational features constitute the *enabling environment* within which organizations develop the *technical skills* needed for effective knowledge sharing.

Creating that enabling environment and developing those technical skills are the subjects of this handbook.

Why Do Organizations Need Knowledge Sharing?

Linking knowledge to action

Drucker (1993, 69) notes that "Knowledge today must prove itself in action." Knowledge becomes an important currency of any organization, equal to the value of productivity or products. Organizations that continue doing business as usual without continuous reflection, learning, course correction, iteration, and the application of solution paths will likely fall behind those that use knowledge to influence how they deliver services.

The ideal organization

If you were to describe your ideal organization, you might think of it as follows:

A complex structure of people who work together using systems and processes to reach a shared goal in the most efficient way.

Taking each part of that description in turn will help clarify the need for knowledge sharing:

> » **Organizations are complex structures.** Even small organizations divide up roles to deal with challenges that must be overcome or at least managed. Successful organizations make sure that "how-to" knowledge is continually shared so that their staff members learn and understand how-to best achieve a given task.

> » **They consist of people.** Organizations have to be mindful of their most important asset—their people. How they communicate, team up to solve problems, get excited about goals and tasks, and deal with adversity will largely determine the performance of the organization. For employees to be well equipped with the knowledge of their peers, everyone in the organization will need to start sharing "how-to" knowledge.

> » **These people work together toward a shared goal.** Although roles must be divided, successful organizations do not let them form into silos that operate at the expense of coordination and collaboration. To most effectively connect and harmonize the different parts of the organization, operating knowledge needs to be

Box I.1 Clarifying Terminology

"Knowledge sharing" and a number of other concepts used in this guide are specialized terms. This handbook contains a glossary, but it is worth extracting from it some basic terms at the outset.

Knowledge capturing

The process of converting the knowledge or experience that resides in the mind of an individual into an explicit representation, whether in print, electronic, or multimedia form.

Knowledge management

A discipline that promotes an integrated approach to identifying, capturing, evaluating, retrieving, and sharing all of an enterprise's knowledge assets. As defined by the Gartner Group (Duhon 1998), these assets include databases, documents, policies, procedures, and previously uncaptured expertise and experience of individual workers. Knowledge management efforts overlap with organizational learning but may be distinguished from that by a greater focus on knowledge as a strategic asset and on encouraging the sharing of knowledge. It is an enabler of organizational learning.

Knowledge sharing

A subset of knowledge management encompassing the exchange of knowledge (information, skills, experiences, or expertise) within and across organizations. Although it can be one-directional, knowledge sharing in most cases is a two-way or multilateral exchange in which the parties learn from each other. Knowledge sharing is more than mere communication, because much knowledge in organizations is hard to articulate. In development work, some knowledge sharing has a regional aspect. For example, South-South knowledge sharing refers to exchanges among partners and peers across developing countries.

Learning organization

"An organization that is skilled at creating, acquiring, and transferring knowledge and at modifying behavior to reflect new knowledge and insights" (Dubrin 2005, 410). As defined by Peter Senge, learning organizations exhibit five main characteristics: personal mastery, mental models, a shared vision, team learning, and—the fifth, integrative characteristic—systems thinking (Senge 2006).

Organizational learning

An area of knowledge within organizational theory that studies how an organization learns and adapts. It is also defined as "a system of actions, actors, symbols, and processes that enable an organization to transform information into valued knowledge, which in turn increases its long-run adaptive capacity" (Schwandt 1994, 58). "Organizational Learning involves making tacit theories of action explicit so that people can become aware of, critically examine, and change them . . . [It] facilitates accountability by increasing self-awareness and enhancing the ability to exercise conscious choice and intention" (Lipshitz, Friedman, and Popper 2007, 122). And "to increase the organization's readiness one must develop the capability to learn how to learn. Policy, structures, and skills are needed to do so" (Schön 1975).

Tacit knowledge, explicit knowledge, and implicit or experiential knowledge

The literature on knowledge management usually distinguishes between tacit (hard to express) knowledge that resides in people's heads and explicit (readily documented) knowledge. Polanyi (1966) proposes the following definitions of tacit and explicit knowledge: "Tacit knowledge is personal, context-specific, and therefore hard to formalize and communicate; explicit knowledge, or 'codified' knowledge, on the other hand, refers to knowledge that can be transmitted by formal systematic language" (cited in Schwandt and Marquardt 1999, 127). As Zack (1999, 46) notes:

> Tacit knowledge is subconsciously understood and applied, difficult to articulate, developed from direct experience and action and usually shared through highly interactive conversation, storytelling, and shared experience. In contrast, explicit knowledge is more precisely and formally articulated, although removed from the original context of creation or use (e.g. an abstract mathematical formula derived from physical experiments or a training manual describing how to close a sale).

These definitions may oversimplify the distinction between knowledge that can be collected and documented (explicit) and knowledge that is difficult to share (tacit). In this handbook we use a third category, *implicit or experiential*, which stands for knowledge that resides in people's heads (including knowledge derived from experience) but which can be converted into explicit knowledge through a process of documentation and capturing (figure I.1.1).

Figure I.1.1 Forms of Knowledge

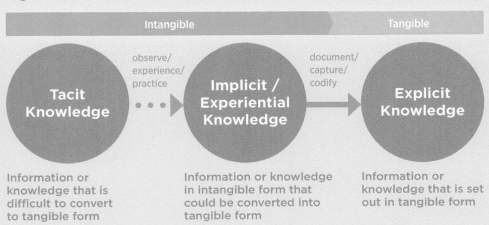

Intangible | Tangible

Tacit Knowledge — observe/experience/practice → Implicit / Experiential Knowledge — document/capture/codify → Explicit Knowledge

Information or knowledge that is difficult to convert to tangible form

Information or knowledge in intangible form that could be converted into tangible form

Information or knowledge that is set out in tangible form

Figure I.1   The Flow of Knowledge Sharing

shared continuously across organizational groups. Successful practices within the organization will be replicated by others; activities with low or no returns will be avoided.

» ***Processes and systems facilitate the work.*** Organizations need processes to facilitate transactions between people, and they develop systems that support these processes. Successful organizations will not only worry about what to do when it comes to procedures but also how best to execute them—and that takes knowledge sharing. So they establish systems and processes to remember, share—and avoid!—actions and experiences that led to negative outcomes and to build on the successes.

Many organizations also deal with other domestic or international constituents and partners that have critical knowledge to share or receive. Successful organizations think carefully about how knowledge can flow more effectively between them and their external stakeholders and apply targeted approaches appropriate for each level—internal, domestic, and international (figure I.1).

Why Is Knowledge Sharing Important in the Context of Development?

Organizations in developing countries that make policy or deliver services heavily influence the quality of life throughout the country. These organizations—for agriculture, health care, disaster relief, and other sectors—have accumulated a wealth of experience with policies and development pathways, but typically they have not been able to retain their experience in ways that allow it to be shared and built upon. Important lessons learned are not documented and get lost along the way. They want to

Figure I.2   Three Typical Knowledge-Related Problems and Knowledge-Sharing Goals for Organizations

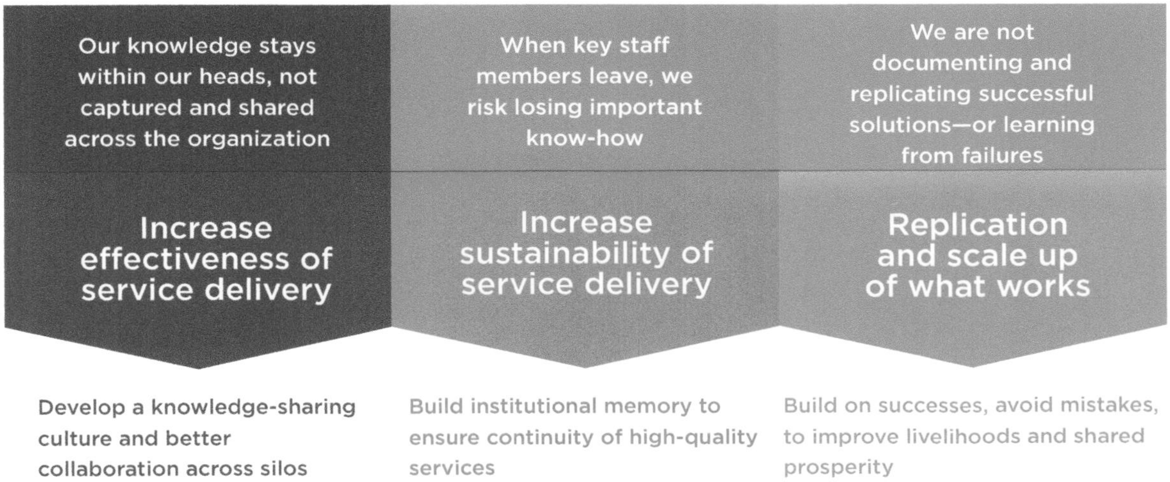

Our knowledge stays within our heads, not captured and shared across the organization	When key staff members leave, we risk losing important know-how	We are not documenting and replicating successful solutions—or learning from failures
Increase effectiveness of service delivery	**Increase sustainability of service delivery**	**Replication and scale up of what works**
Develop a knowledge-sharing culture and better collaboration across silos	Build institutional memory to ensure continuity of high-quality services	Build on successes, avoid mistakes, to improve livelihoods and shared prosperity

strengthen their abilities for capturing, learning from, and sharing their knowledge and experiences and reap the benefits. In particular, they typically want to accomplish three goals (figure I.2):

» Become more effective. With access to critical knowledge when and where needed, organizations accelerate operational processes and avoid mistakes

» Maintain a high level of institutional knowledge even when key staff members depart

» Solve operational problems by continually evaluating and taking to scale what worked in isolated instances and avoiding what didn't

The Heart of This Guide: A Framework for Developing Knowledge-Sharing Capabilities

For knowledge sharing to thrive, organizations need to develop two very different types of *capability enabling environment* and *technical skills*. The enabling environment is created largely by strategic decisions made by management of the organization. The technical skills operationalize effective knowledge capturing and sharing. Each capability can be divided into four pillars (figure I.3).

You will see that successful knowledge-sharing organizations have built their capability on a large foundation—eight pillars supporting organizational traits and technical skills—without which knowledge sharing cannot become a powerful institutional force.

Figure I.3   The Eight Pillars of the Knowledge-Sharing Capabilities Framework

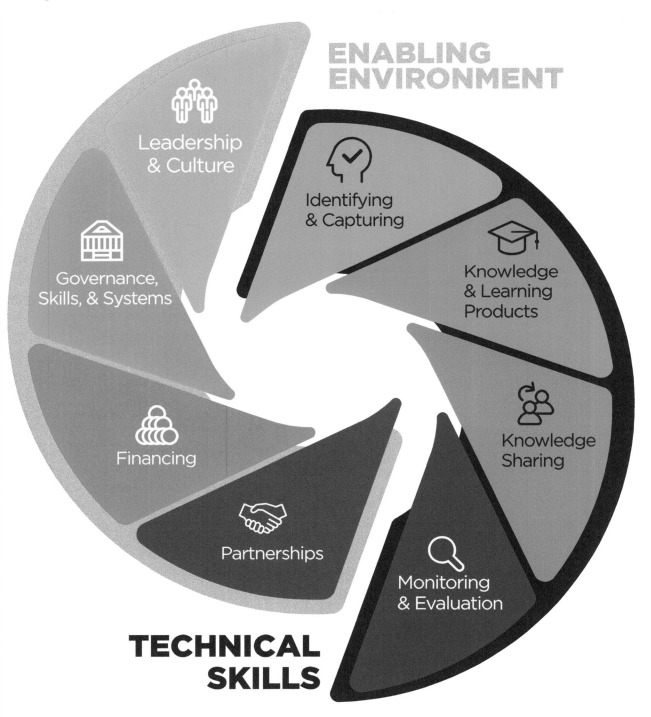

Enabling environment

A positive enabling environment consists of **(1) leadership and an organizational culture** conducive to knowledge sharing. The environment builds on strong leadership by senior management that treats knowledge and learning as part of everyday operations and includes attractive recognition mechanisms that reward staff for sharing. It includes **(2) effective governance mechanisms** for knowledge- and learning-related issues and a set of policies that guide the institution on its journey to becoming a learning organization. The environment is supported by **(3) financing** and by **(4) partnerships**, both domestic and international.

Technical skills

Technical capabilities for effective knowledge operations consist of systematically **(5) identifying and capturing** the organization's operational experiences and lessons, **(6)** packaging them into **knowledge and learning products**, **(7) sharing** them within and outside the institution, and **(8) monitoring and evaluating** these efforts.

These eight characteristics are the framework for this handbook. The following chapters will help your institution adapt them to its own circumstances and join the ranks of knowledge-sharing organizations.

1. LEADERSHIP AND CULTURE

Knowledge Sharing in Action

Inducing Systematic Knowledge Sharing and Collaboration

DANE, the National Statistics Agency of Colombia

DANE, Colombia's National Administrative Department of Statistics, administers the national census every five years, tracks the country's national accounts, and maintains data on demographic and economic indicators. Because it was being increasingly recognized as an important reference organization in its field, DANE realized it would need to work on its own organizational culture more intentionally to promote the values of openness and collaboration to its staff.

DANE therefore created "DANE Moderno" (Modern DANE), an initiative that includes stronger cross-departmental collaboration and knowledge sharing to improve the way the organization does business. True to its goals, DANE Moderno itself was developed collaboratively by senior management and staff members throughout the organization.

In consultation with the staff, DANE's senior and midlevel management drafted a vision statement in which DANE would become "a center of excellence in knowledge management for the production and sharing of official statistics at the internal, national, and international level" within five years. Next, they launched a capacity assessment that identified assets to build on and gaps to be addressed. An action plan provided a timeline for achieving the five-year vision, which included developing a cross-departmental knowledge management team, a set of knowledge management policies, and technical capacities for knowledge capturing, packaging, and sharing.

DANE thereafter began sharing knowledge both within the organization and with external partners and peer institutions in a systematic way. A year after the launch of DANE Moderno, staff members reported a greater motivation to share their experiences with each other and a strong sense of pride in being an active part of successful results. Internally, DANE has formalized knowledge-sharing events, such as regular "learning from experience" sessions that allow staff members to share results of their latest projects. Externally, the organization has significantly improved the way it shares its knowledge with foreign peer organizations by responding directly to specific requests.

1.1   Why Are Leadership and a Knowledge-Sharing Culture Important?

Here are some key characteristics of an organization with a strong knowledge-sharing culture:

» Everyone in the organization understands the strategic importance of knowledge.

» Leaders promote collaboration and knowledge sharing throughout the organization.

» Leaders celebrate knowledge sharing.

» Knowledge sharing is embedded in the organization's vision and strategy.

An organization's culture is a complex interplay of many factors, including the organization's history, style of leadership, external environment, financial situation, governance structure, mission, and values. Perhaps those conditions in your organization will inhibit a belief that "sharing knowledge is power" and constrain efforts to make knowledge accessible to everyone who can contribute to it or use it. Knowledge flows best when people trust each other, and it is trust that will overcome both a resistance to ask for advice and a resistance to sharing personal experiences with peers.

Where to begin the change? There is no blueprint for creating a knowledge-sharing organization, but experience shows that it will not happen without strong leadership and a supportive environment to guide the behavior of the people who make up the organization. After all, knowledge sharing and learning are social activities. Providing a positive atmosphere for knowledge sharing can set the foundation for a change of culture. It will not happen overnight, but senior management can provide the fertile ground for it to happen. So we begin with leadership.

How people begin to change their behavior will be tied to how the organization motivates and acknowledges them. Senior management's explicit and implicit expectations will determine whether people will voluntarily share their knowledge as part of their daily work, or see it as a secondary responsibility, or, indeed, even see it as a threat to their success. Any effort to induce knowledge sharing without the commitment of the organization's senior management is likely to fail.

Know what you know. Most organizations are already at least partly engaged in some good knowledge-sharing practices without even realizing it. Look for teams or groups that are sharing knowledge and find out how their processes are benefiting both the team and the organization as a whole. Celebrate these examples of good practice and use them to inform your knowledge-sharing strategy.

1.2   Key Elements of Transformation for Knowledge Sharing

This chapter highlights four key elements of any program to transform the workplace into a knowledge-sharing organization.

1. Leadership: Ensuring senior management buy-in and support

2. Vision and expectations: Making knowledge sharing the default behavior

3. Strategy: Designing knowledge-sharing initiatives

4. Incentives: Updating organizational and personnel policies and recognition of champions

1.2.1   Leadership

Knowledge sharing starts at the top, but even managers who support it might still need some coaching. The behaviors it requires may well be as new to them as to everyone else. Some knowledge-sharing practitioners have also found it useful to start with a pilot project first, before asking supervisors for long-term commitments.

Let's look at a few concrete measures both to persuade senior management and to exercise leadership for knowledge sharing.

Build buy-in at the top

Senior management will play a vital role in the design, rollout, and scale up of the knowledge-sharing strategy. So, if any senior managers are skeptical about the merits of systematic knowledge sharing, they must be convinced before the program is launched throughout the organization. But how do you convince the skeptics? Here is where pilot programs are useful, because one powerful way to persuade is to show how knowledge sharing has helped a unit or team deliver on its work program.

Act as role models at the top

Management must promote the value of sound and systematic knowledge sharing by modeling best-practice behaviors. This will signal the strategic importance of the investment to all colleagues. Managers who engage in nontransparent decision making will likely be less effective in introducing a new paradigm such as knowledge sharing than if they model collaborative processes and open communications. Staff will also take their cues from how your organization's managers encourage, recognize, and reward knowledge sharing. Simple examples of managers practicing what they preach include regular letters to staff, participatory townhall meetings, staff retreats, and active participation in knowledge-sharing activities.

Start with knowledge sharing in the senior management team, and ask the team members to directly communicate and discuss the decisions and results in their departments. Smith and McKeen (2003) suggest that managers should foster knowledge sharing in the organization through questions such as "Who have you shared this with?" and "Who else can make use of this information?"[1]

---

[1]   Cited in Lipshitz, Friedman, and Popper (2007, 104).

Embed knowledge sharing in the senior management team

To integrate knowledge sharing in the organization, anchor it in the senior management team or even create direct reporting lines to the head of the organization. Some organizations choose to establish a "chief knowledge and learning officer," others embed knowledge and learning as part of the competencies of the chief operations officer. Bringing on board midlevel management is also necessary to ensure strong uptake in all departments, but beware of putting the information technology (IT) or communications department in charge. The danger there is alienating the staff of core operations departments, who might conclude that knowledge capture and sharing is a support function, not a core function. (Specific roles and structures are presented in greater detail in chapter 2.)

Identify knowledge-sharing champions

Forge a broad coalition of champions who have taken ownership of the new agenda and who take pride in inspiring others. Every organization has champions. They may not be highly placed on the organization chart, but they are the staff members that colleagues look to for guidance and whose signals can influence individual behavior. They exercise informal leadership. As role models in their own right, these champions should be enlisted as part of the change to a knowledge-sharing culture. Other natural allies are colleagues in the human resources function and any staff members tasked with knowledge management and learning.

Communicate, communicate, communicate

Communications and branding are critical to the success of any change-management process. Involving stakeholders in the discussions early on will pay off in the form of stronger buy-in because staff will experience being part of the process. Give the knowledge-sharing initiative a creative and inspiring name and continue communicating about it regularly with all stakeholders. Depending on accepted practice in your organization, use flyers, posters, e-mail, web newsletters, blog posts, and fun events to build momentum. As Lipshitz, Friedman, and Popper (2007, 103) point out, having management proactively communicate about the importance of knowledge sharing and organizational learning can be highly valuable.

Make a compelling business case. For senior management and other leaders in the organization to be fully on board it is useful to make a compelling business case for knowledge sharing. What concrete business challenges can it address? How can it contribute to improving service delivery or policy implementation? Anchoring knowledge sharing in some (or all) of the core operations of an organization will help people see its value.

1.2.2   Vision and expectations

Establishing a culture of knowledge sharing means that it has to become the default behavior across your organization. A clear understanding that knowledge sharing is a standard institutional practice should be reflected in the words and actions of leaders, in the definition of roles and responsibilities (discussed in chapter 2), and in performance evaluations and rewards. Time spent capturing and sharing knowledge needs to be recognized as "real work"—an integral part of everyone's job that is valued by the organization. Employees need to be given time to seek out knowledge, reflect on it, and share what they know.

When do you know you are successful? There is no particular threshold for becoming a knowledge-sharing organization, but quite a few indicators will point you toward "getting it right" (table 1.1).

Table 1.1 Indicators of Success in Building a Knowledge-Sharing Culture

Characteristic	Traditional Organization	Knowledge-Sharing Organization
Leadership behavior	Senior management sees knowledge sharing as the business of the communications and IT departments. Decisions are announced to staff, not explained. Opportunities for staff to contribute through sharing experiences are not provided.	Senior management models knowledge sharing, for example by practicing open communication, organizing participatory meetings, and sharing its relevant experiences with staff.
Recognition	The organization sees knowledge sharing as separate from core operations.	The organization recognizes knowledge sharing as a valuable behavior that improves organizational performance in the core business.
Systems and processes	The organization provides only limited means for knowledge sharing to happen.	Systems, platforms, and processes that foster systematic knowledge sharing are actively used by the members of the organization.
Collaboration	Collaboration among individuals and teams is not actively encouraged or supported.	Teams are rewarded for collaboration that leads to faster or better results.
Governance	Roles and responsibilities for knowledge sharing have not been defined. Knowledge-sharing is the business of a few staff in IT or in the learning department.	Clear roles and responsibilities have been embedded throughout the organization for critical tasks related to knowledge capturing, sharing, and learning, and knowledge sharing is understood to be everybody's business.
Skills	The organization has no means to identify, capture, store, and share operationally relevant experiences and lessons learned.	The necessary technical skills are in place to deliver on vital knowledge-sharing functions. Tools for identifying, capturing, storing, and sharing are widely used throughout the organization.
Financing	The organization has not developed a dedicated budget for knowledge management.	The organization budgets for knowledge management.
Networks and partnerships	The organization does not see partners and networks as a valuable source of knowledge to improve its operations.	The organization uses knowledge-sharing networks and partnerships to improve its operations.
Systematic capturing	The members of the organization do not systematically document experiences and lessons learned.	The members of the organization contribute to the organization's knowledge repository by regularly posting experiences and lessons learned.
Accessibility	Knowledge and how-to guidance is difficult to find in the organization.	Knowledge needed by members of the organization is made easily and readily available in a just-in-time, just-when-needed and just-where-needed manner.
Learning	Predominantly lecture-based training is the primary format for learning offerings in the organization. The content of learning offerings is largely generic, not customized.	Participatory offerings engage the learner through a variety of action-oriented activities. The content is customized to the specific needs of the learners.
Opportunities	The organization has not developed formal spaces for knowledge sharing and relies on informal knowledge sharing to happen when and where needed.	The organization provides time and (physical or virtual) space to engage in knowledge sharing, for example through dedicated events. Informal knowledge sharing is encouraged, for example through open-space architecture and extracurricular activities.
Measuring results	The organization does not monitor or evaluate its knowledge sharing.	Knowledge capturing and sharing are continuously monitored and evaluated to improve quality of outcomes and operational relevance.

Perhaps the biggest indication of success is when knowledge sharing and learning start to happen naturally as part of core operations. Staff members will share because they want to, not because they have to. Knowledge sharing becomes valued as a key way of doing business. It becomes part of the organization's DNA.

Develop the vision collaboratively. A vision that comes only from the top is not likely to get the level of buy-in you can achieve by establishing it jointly with key stakeholders throughout the organization. Involve champions at all levels who can take the message to colleagues and partners to generate enthusiasm and excitement about the new agenda.

1.2.3   Strategy

An organization's leadership is tasked with developing the strategy that will steer the organization toward a shared vision. A clear strategy will guide you in designing your knowledge-sharing initiatives, inform all stakeholders in the organization about the value of knowledge sharing, and facilitate the dissemination of your strategy across your organization.

A good knowledge-sharing strategy will help achieve the following goals:

» Provide a clear, communicable plan about where your organization is, where it needs to go, and how to get there

» Generate and confirm senior leadership commitment

» Increase awareness and understanding across the organization

» Attract people and resources to help implement and scale up activities

A good strategy document will have the following characteristics:

» Use clear language to enable widespread understanding

» Provide inspiring principles rather than paralyzing processes

» Set direction without dictating operational detail

» Create a framework that others can follow with natural connections to their established work flow

Here are important elements of the strategy document:

1. **Preamble.** Links the knowledge-sharing agenda of the organization to the overarching values of the organization and its overall mission.

2. **Vision and expectations.** Sets the goals and expectations of the organization regarding knowledge sharing. It defines what success would look like once systematic knowledge-sharing practices have been instituted.

3. **Guiding principles.** Describes the key principles that will guide the organization's knowledge-sharing practices.

4. **Stakeholders.** Identifies the stakeholders that would be actors or beneficiaries of sound knowledge-sharing practices and describes their needs. A critical component of a knowledge-sharing strategy, it helps target knowledge-sharing policies and practices.

5. **Policies and practices.** The core of the document, laying out critical policies and the policies that implement them. The structure of this section will depend on your organization's needs. One possibility is to organize it according to the eight pillars of the knowledge-sharing capabilities framework described in the introduction (see figure I.3). A variation of that approach is to separately view the eight pillars from the internal, domestic, and international perspectives. Another possibility for structuring this section is to map policies and practices to core business processes.

6. **Implementation.** The steps needed to implement the change-management process that will establish knowledge sharing throughout the organization. Here are some components to consider:

   a. **Timeline.** The timeline can come in two levels of detail—a high-level overview and a detailed schedule of tasks. The overview provides the critical implementation milestones, and the detailed schedule gives clear time requirements, deadlines, and responsibilities. Each level can be portrayed in a table format or through a Gantt chart

   b. **Governance.** Governance material defines the decision makers, implementers, and reporting lines and describes the mechanisms for guidance and implementation

   c. **Roles and responsibilities.** More detail on the roles and responsibilities and required capacities of the various stakeholder groups that will implement the knowledge-sharing strategy

   d. **Budget.** The financial needs of the implementation strategy. The financial data should be fairly detailed for the first year but can be more high-level for subsequent years, when priorities and implementation actions will likely be influenced by experiences in the first year.

7. **Accessibility and a summary version.** Accessibility is a key element of communication. The complete strategy document may be comprehensive and address various organizational considerations, but being concise and avoiding excessive detail are still important. In addition, a single two-sided sheet or folded four-page sheet capturing the key concepts and elements of your strategy and its expected benefits will be invaluable; get it endorsed at the highest level of the organization and disseminate it widely.

Co-create the strategy document. Involve a broad set of stakeholders and champions in drafting the strategy. Doing so will help build ownership and excitement by creating a shared agenda rather than simply issuing a directive.

1.2.4   Incentives

Knowledge Sharing in Action

Rewarding Knowledge-Sharing Behavior

Lagos Metropolitan Area Transport Authority, Nigeria

The Lagos Metropolitan Area Transport Authority (LAMATA) was established in 2002 to comprehensively manage and upgrade all public transportation service in Lagos, one of the world's megacities. With little ability to reward staff financially, LAMATA's management seeks to systematically foster knowledge sharing through a variety of nonmonetary rewards. Staff members are encouraged to share their knowledge through different platforms that provide visibility and recognition. They are also rewarded with educational opportunities such as management courses and participation at international seminars.

Successful organizations have recognized the critical value of collaboration and collective deliverables for achieving best results. Therefore, they encourage and acknowledge proactive knowledge sharing and collaboration across functional and organizational boundaries. Given that many employees see their knowledge as an asset that gives them an edge over their colleagues, devising incentives is critical to making knowledge sharing a standard behavior.

Lipshitz, Friedman, and Popper (2007, 112) point out that

> successful dissemination hinges on the motivation of people to share their knowledge and the credibility that they enjoy among potential recipients. The motivation of the source is clearly influenced by self-interest. After all, dissemination involves costs to the source. To the extent that knowledge is seen as power, people who share knowledge give away a potentially valuable asset. Depending on the precise mode that sharing knowledge takes, they may also have to divert time and energy from their own work in order to document their knowledge, explain it to others, or coach them in its implementation. Thus, people who are sources have to believe that they will benefit—or at least not be hurt—from sharing knowledge.

Research has shown that a behavior change toward the better use of knowledge and learning is inherently influenced by the biases of staff and management. The World Bank's Independent Evaluation Group (IEG), in its reviews of the organization's ability to reflect on and learn from its operations, has identified six major biases that staff members need to overcome.[2] Similarly, Gino and Staats

---

[2]   These are simplification bias, confirmation bias, self-serving bias, champion bias, sunk-cost bias, and subjectivity bias (IEG 2014 and 2015).

(2015) point out that people in organizations struggle with several common challenges that hinder them from engaging in reflection and collaboration.[3]

Given these behavioral biases, designing the right incentives and rewards to promote knowledge sharing requires striking a balance between intrinsic (encompassing inward satisfaction) and extrinsic (materially oriented) forms of incentives (box 1.1). Some staff will quickly ask for monetary rewards, although as a stand-alone measure, these may not be the most effective for achieving sustainable behavior change. As is often the case with material incentives, once you stop them, behaviors may slip back into older habits. Examples of extrinsic rewards that are often more effective include special learning opportunities and fast-tracked promotion. But many colleagues in your organization will be motivated most by receiving recognition and visibility, and others may simply value sharing and receiving knowledge for its own sake.

Box 1.1 Clarifying Terminology: Motivations and Incentives

Extrinsic motivation refers to the "tendency to perform activities for known external rewards, whether they be tangible (e.g. money) or psychological (e.g. praise) in nature" (Brown 2007, 143). Extrinsic rewards can include recognition, honors, pay raises, bonuses, training, and career development.

Intrinsic motivation refers to behavior based on intangible rewards that arise from an individual's own personal values and motivations. They can include a sense of accomplishment, pride, and satisfaction derived from completing a challenging task or from the pursuit of learning. They are not necessarily tied to achieving a specific objective.

Many common intrinsic and extrinsic incentives vary in terms of the resource intensity their implementation would require (figure 1.1). In the initial stages of knowledge sharing, informal rewards and recognition, such as showcasing staff expertise in visible ways, may be most effective, especially where knowledge sharing is not the default behavior among staff members. Your organization should use a mix of incentives appropriate to your culture and context.

Ultimately, working with the human resources department in crafting policies and practices will be essential in developing an appropriate incentive system. Making knowledge-sharing part of each job's terms of reference and including it as part of the performance review can also be a driver for knowledge-sharing behavior. The clearer the definition of the targets at the outset, the easier it is to measure against them at the end of a performance review cycle. Using the performance review system helps reveal how well staff members share knowledge, signals that it is important to the organization, and guides the improvement of staff practices. The performance review system is discussed more in chapter 8, in the context of monitoring and evaluation.

---

[3] They tend to be risk averse out of fear of failure, focus on their own immediate and recent past performance instead of their potential for improvement, and fail to learn from past mistakes (which they attribute to unfortunate circumstances).

Figure 1.1   Incentives, by Type and Resource Intensity

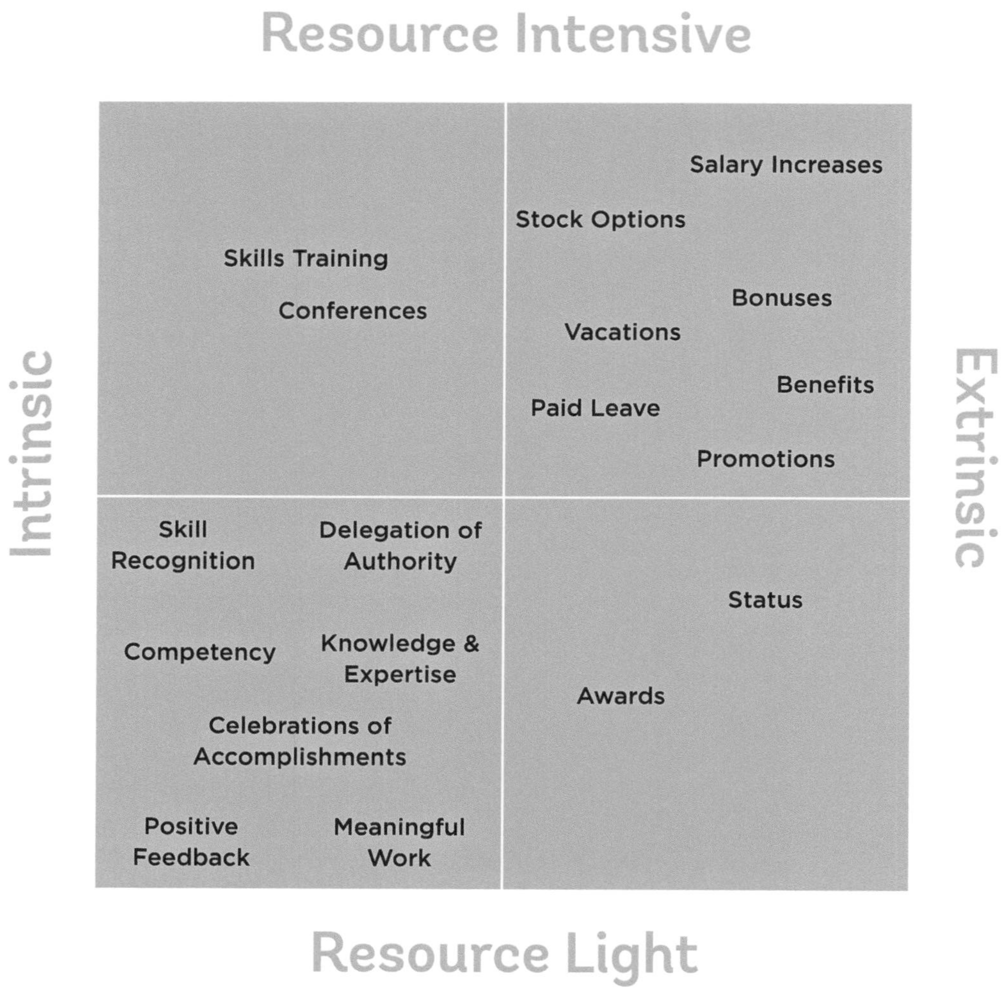

Resource Intensive

Skills Training **Conferences**	**Salary Increases** **Stock Options** **Bonuses** **Vacations** **Benefits** **Paid Leave** **Promotions**
Skill Recognition **Delegation of Authority** **Competency** **Knowledge & Expertise** **Celebrations of Accomplishments** **Positive Feedback** **Meaningful Work**	**Status** **Awards**

Intrinsic ← → *Extrinsic*

Resource Light

Showcase the good rather than shame the bad. Strategies to change an organization's culture by naming and shaming "bad" practices will not win over many supporters. Instead, working *within* your organization's culture, highlight even small success stories. Senior management's promotion of these success stories will lend validity to them and can lead to a "snowball effect" as more employees carry out these practices.

1.3 Conclusion

A leadership committed to knowledge sharing must see knowledge as a strategic asset, develop a clear vision of how people in the organization should behave, and champion that vision. Culture cannot be changed overnight, but organizations can put in place a variety of measures to gradually shift their culture toward becoming more open and collaborative.

1.4 Checklist

Leadership and Culture	Yes
Does our senior management team see knowledge sharing as an important success factor for delivering on our mandate?	
Is knowledge sharing linked to concrete deliverables?	
Do our managers act as role models for knowledge-sharing behavior?	
Do our managers encourage and acknowledge outstanding knowledge-sharing behavior?	
Are staff members and teams rewarded or acknowledged for collaborative behavior?	
Do members of our organization trust each other enough to ask questions and provide sincere support to get to solutions?	
Is knowledge sharing part of everyone's job description?	
Is knowledge sharing discussed during performance reviews?	
Do we have a knowledge and learning strategy for our organization?	

2. GOVERNANCE STRUCTURES AND SYSTEMS

Knowledge Sharing in Action

Setting Up a Governance Mechanism for Learning and Knowledge Sharing

Nigeria's Federal Ministry of Agriculture and Rural Development

In Nigeria, more than 70 percent of the poor are dependent on agricultural production, a sector plagued by high costs for seeds and fertilizer and low productivity. For many years, the high costs and the corruption in the distribution of subsidized seed and fertilizer meant that, for example, only 11 percent of farmers in Nigeria used fertilizer to boost their yields.

In 2011, the Nigerian government eliminated subsidized distribution and replaced it with the Growth Enhancement Scheme (GES). The GES allows the market to set prices while providing a 50 percent subsidy to farmers on a seasonal maximum of two bags of fertilizer and one bag of seeds. To deliver the subsidy directly rather than through middlemen, the program established "e-wallet," an electronic voucher mechanism based on national identification records and distributed via mobile phones. The farmers use the vouchers to receive the subsidized inputs at their local dealer. In addition, the ministry built a mobile web application accessible to private and public sector stakeholders providing news and policy information that before had been essentially impossible to distribute so widely in timely fashion.

To preserve and learn from the rich experience of designing and implementing these initiatives, the Federal Ministry of Agriculture and Rural Development (FMARD) in 2014 asked the United Nations Development Programme and the World Bank for help in developing a knowledge-management program for the ministry and its GES partners. The knowledge-management program would also be used with the stakeholders of the ministry's broader Agricultural Transformation Agenda.

FMARD identified the critical areas requiring attention through a set of workshops involving all stakeholder groups over a four-month period. One of six areas agreed on for priority action was creating a governance mechanism for knowledge management (KM). The KM governance structure created for the GES program consisted of (1) supervision by the existing GES Working Group and (2) implementation by a new KM Working Group.

As the GES program was being developed, the GES Working Group, its governing body, brought together up to 70 stakeholders each week to review progress. Initially chaired by the Minister of Agriculture and Rural Development to demonstrate high-level leadership, the meetings have since become well established and are run by a director in the ministry.

The KM Working Group consists of two members from each of the ministry's 18 departments. It is chaired by the deputy director of the ministry's planning department, which plays a key role in the implementation of the ministry's overall strategy. The KM Working Group meets regularly and reports back once a month to the GES Working Group.

2.1 Why Are Governance Structures and Systems Important for Knowledge Sharing?

As discussed in chapter 1, senior management should develop a clear vision and strategy for knowledge sharing. But the *practice* of knowledge sharing cannot be taken for granted. It will not happen without specific structures, systems, and roles to support it. So the next step is to establish these supporting features. This may mean more resources or additional structures, but often just rearranging and making efficient use of what is already available will suffice. In any case, a good governance structure guides but does not stifle. It is a framework for action that leaves the detailed procedures and processes to the leaders who are implementing the work.

Knowledge sharing is at the crossroads of core and support functions. The knowledge being shared is typically that of the core operational departments, but knowledge sharing needs the involvement of knowledge and learning support staff to ensure maintenance of the knowledge management process.

In general, senior management will have to decide on who will oversee and implement the organization's knowledge sharing and learning program, and those functions in turn will have to establish the necessary strategies, roles, and responsibilities. Large institutions organized on a hierarchical model can set up many knowledge-sharing positions (figure 2.1). You may not need all of these functions. Some organizations may instead assign knowledge and learning directly to the head of the organization and develop a federated model in which all departments work on knowledge-sharing targets (figure 2.2). Small organizations at times embed the knowledge function in the human resources or communications department.

For many organizations, knowledge sharing is a relatively new function. Knowledge-sharing job titles vary, and organizational charts may not accurately reflect the knowledge-sharing work that people are actually doing. While one person may have a title such as knowledge officer, people in many other positions—including operational roles such as regional coordinator or program officer—may bear much of the responsibility for knowledge work.

Figure 2.1 Knowledge-Sharing Governance and Roles: Hierarchical Structure

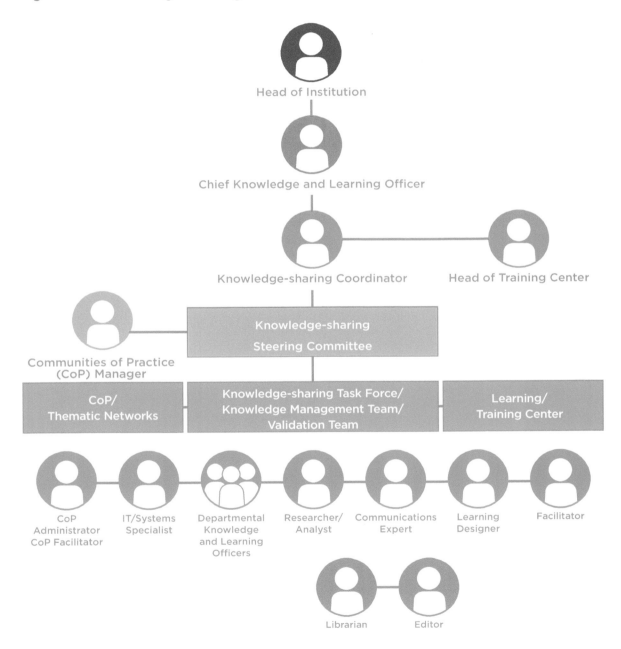

Figure 2.2   Knowledge-Sharing Governance and Roles: Federated Structure

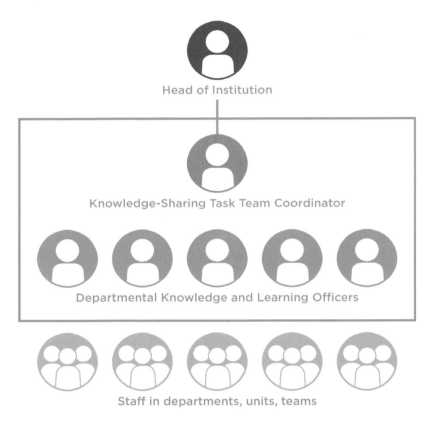

Knowledge-Sharing Task Force/
Knowledge Management Team/
Validation Team

The following sections give a broad overview of the elements that determine an effective knowledge-sharing culture:

» Organizational structures and staffing

» Strategic issues in the use of experts and outsourcing

» Roles and responsibilities

» Skills and training

» Knowledge management systems

Governance should evolve over time. Governance must not be static—you can't just set it and forget it. If mechanisms do not evolve in response to changing organizational circumstances, they risk becoming irrelevant or, worse, a barrier to progress. For example, a weekly meeting of a large interdepartmental steering committee may be essential at the outset to get processes and systems established. But the size and mandate of the group and the frequency of its meetings should be adjusted as circumstances change.

2.2   Organizational Structures and Staffing

Getting ready for large-scale knowledge sharing means creating a strong yet flexible operational set-up that mobilizes and improves internal capacities. Organizations around the world have learned important lessons about what organizational structures for knowledge sharing suits them best—no single model ensures success.

You may be able to modify structures that already exist; for example, an established working group previously focused on communications might evolve to take on stewardship for knowledge sharing. When feasible, however, it will be useful to develop a governance arrangement consisting of two levels: (1) *supervision* by a steering committee representing the entire organization and chaired by a member of senior management and (2) *implementation* by a team of knowledge and learning specialists headed by a member of senior management.

2.2.1   Supervision: The knowledge-sharing steering committee

Many organizations create a steering committee to manage the change process for knowledge sharing. It is best led by a member of the senior management team who is a proven champion of the agenda. Its membership should be drawn from departments throughout the organization to demonstrate the scope of the initiative: knowledge sharing and learning are everyone's business, and the committee needs to reflect that.

The responsibilities of the knowledge-sharing steering committee include some or all of the following elements:

- » Devising an organizational strategy for knowledge sharing
- » Supervising the knowledge-sharing change process
- » Appointing an implementation team and its leader
- » Approving knowledge-sharing partnerships

» Ensuring that operational units are aligned with support functions in their implementation of knowledge sharing

» Supporting and regularly briefing senior management on all knowledge-sharing issues

2.2.2   Implementation

Knowledge management coordination team

In larger organizations with a knowledge-sharing steering committee, the implementation of the committee's agenda may be assigned to a knowledge management team headed by a chief knowledge and learning officer.

The knowledge management team is composed of knowledge and learning specialists who provide coordination and training and facilitate activities via seed resources, expertise, and project management. The team monitors the organization's knowledge-sharing activities and feeds performance reports back to the knowledge-sharing steering committee.

Chief knowledge and learning officer

The chief knowledge and learning officer is a member of senior management and is its point of contact for all implementation issues. The officer oversees development of all major support tools and systems, knowledge-sharing partnerships, and information access restrictions. In some small organizations, the officer is the institution's chief executive.

Larger organizations find it useful to support and extend the reach of the chief knowledge and learning officer by assigning corresponding duties to staff members at the team or department level. Such personnel are often best placed to identify operationally relevant experiences and to document them in easily accessible knowledge assets for further sharing and replication.

Learning and training center

Knowledge sharing is all about learning. Many organizations with a large-scale knowledge-sharing agenda have a learning and training center to support it. The center's staff should include experts with the skill to translate knowledge into suitable learning offerings and the ability to organize knowledge-sharing events and gatherings, including with external partners.

Communities of practice

Communities of practice (also known as expert networks) are peer networks of practitioners in a given problem area or field who help each other perform better by sharing their knowledge. A community manager is usually designated to ensure that the community functions effectively. A community facilitator may also be assigned to provide day-to-day assistance to community members. Managing knowledge sharing exclusively by instituting communities of practice requires an advanced level of organizational maturity and strong incentives for staff to actively participate on an ongoing basis.

But regardless of whether your organization adopts all or none of the above functions, knowledge sharing and learning must become everyone's business. Only if everyone in the organization sees themselves as both a source and recipient of knowledge will the culture take root and the organization benefit.

2.3 Strategic Issues: Using Experts and Outsourcing While Building an In-House Culture

2.3.1 Use of experts

Knowledge and learning needs to be located in the areas of the organization where it is being generated—that is, everywhere. Many organizations make the mistake of thinking that a dedicated team will suffice for knowledge to permeate throughout the organization. But a typical result of that approach is that the rest of the staff members rely solely on their dedicated team and do not think of knowledge and learning as part of their own job description.

For knowledge and learning to thrive, organizations therefore need to develop two complementary strategies: (1) building a team of knowledge and learning specialists and (2) embedding knowledge and learning in job descriptions so that knowledge and learning becomes everybody's business.

A common question is whether to centralize or decentralize the placement of knowledge and learning specialists. A rule of thumb is that the larger the organization, the more useful it is to place knowledge and learning officers in all departments. These officers would have direct reporting lines to a chief knowledge and learning officer or coordination officer, but they would also report to the heads of their respective operational departments. Their function is to help identify, capture, and package critical experiences and lessons learned from core operations in their departments. In mature organizations, such functions can gradually be taken over by all staff, assuming that appropriate accountability measures have been put in place.

Integrate knowledge-sharing and learning functions as much as possible into core operations. One of the main hurdles blocking creation of a knowledge-sharing culture is the perception that it is a lower-priority add-on to existing job responsibilities. To help overcome that perception, frame knowledge and learning tasks as part of, and integrated into, staff members' day-to-day work. The expectations should be clearly written out in collaboration with upper management.

2.3.2   Use outsourcing or in-house capabilities?

Hiring or developing knowledge and learning specialists may sound like a daunting endeavor for many organizations. A valid question is therefore whether organizations can outsource knowledge and learning to service providers. Outsourcing can have certain advantages: overall staffing (and thus fixed costs) remain lower; new tools and processes provided by vendors can continuously enrich the organization; and creation of new capacities, which can be time consuming, does not have to be conducted in-house.

Some tasks are easier and more appropriate to outsource than others (figure 2.3). For example, developing technical systems and packaging content into learning materials require specific technical skills and may be too costly to perform in-house unless the organization has reached a certain size and maturity. Tasks such as identifying, capturing, and sharing are often kept in-house as these pertain to the core knowledge of the organization. Some organizations choose to get external support for the capturing of experiences, for example through partnerships with universities, where students or recent graduates form capturing teams that support operational teams. Others choose to outsource to private firms that offer this service for a fee. Validation (demonstrating the applicability of the captured knowledge) is a process that can be useful to conduct both as an internal exercise and through external experts, who can bring a fresh and neutral perspective.

Figure 2.3   In-House versus Outsourcing: What Is Most Suitable for Knowledge-Sharing Tasks?

	Function	In-House	External
🔍	Identification	✓	
📄	Capturing	✓	✓
👍	Validation	✓	✓
☁	IT-systems hosting/support	✓	✓
💬	Brokering and sharing	✓	
👥	Communities of practice support	✓	
🎓	Learning design		✓
💡	Training/facilitation	✓	✓

But even where outsourcing makes sense, it can have significant disadvantages. Knowledge and learning can become somewhat more of an add-on activity and less embedded in core organizational practice, which would be detrimental to the knowledge-sharing message that should be conveyed to staff members. An operational difficulty is that the service provider should "shadow" operational staff on a continuous basis. If relying solely on an outsourced partner, it will be difficult to avoid dependency—what will happen to the systems and processes if the contract is not renewed? Overall, learning and knowledge sharing should remain part of what the organization itself does, regardless of any support obtained from an external service provider.

2.4   Roles and Responsibilities

Looking beyond formal titles, it is important to consider the roles that are commonly required to implement knowledge-sharing activities.

Below is a list of possible positions with functions and roles that may be relevant for your organization to consider. The descriptions are illustrative, and should be adapted to fit your organization's context.

Journalist. Captures knowledge by interviewing others or recording key events

Analyst. Identifies and reviews information and effectively synthesizes it into actionable form

Editor. Refines knowledge that has been captured in documents, videos, or other formats and converts it into user-friendly formats or languages

Librarian. Organizes knowledge assets and assists others in locating and navigating them

Facilitator. Assists groups of people to identify and achieve their objectives

Broker. Knows the system—connects those who seek with those who have

Instructional designer. Turns content into accessible learning offerings by designing learning activities using a variety of pedagogical tools

Community-of-practice manager. Administers and manages the community-of-practice platform by engaging with the members and ensuring the offerings on the platform meet their expectations

IT Specialist. Manages and administrates the IT-based platforms and systems

Every organization is different—with different challenges and contexts. Knowledge-sharing functions can and probably should change organically over time. Roles and responsibilities of the core team, in particular, will evolve according to the maturity of your knowledge-sharing program and the resources and approaches you are working with.

2.5   Skills and Training

Knowledge-sharing initiatives will not gain a foothold in an organization's daily operations unless staff members are trained in how to participate in and benefit from knowledge sharing. Including specific knowledge-sharing tasks and responsibilities in staff members' job descriptions and terms of reference is vital to the expansion of knowledge sharing within the organization. To be effective, however, the job descriptions must be preceded and supported by training.

Some of the more commonly required skills are

- » Interpersonal communication
- » Information technology
- » Learning design and facilitation
- » Journalism skills
- » Information management
- » Writing skills
- » Analytical skills
- » Management skills

Make sure the training programs you design relate to the specific tasks and functions your employees already perform. For example, if staff members are expected to use a new blog on the intranet to share after-action reviews, then providing training in effective writing and in the mechanics of creating blog entries will improve both compliance and the quality of the contributions. Integrating knowledge-sharing training in the orientation activities for new hires can also be an effective way to embed knowledge-sharing habits in your organizational culture.

2.6   Using Technology for Knowledge Sharing

Today's ample menu of low-cost and easy-to-access information technology (IT) tools can significantly support meaningful and large-scale knowledge sharing. They provide for agile management of knowledge assets and enable peers to build results-oriented collaborations and long-term partnerships.

However, a common misconception is that knowledge management is primarily about technology. Lessons learned over the years have demonstrated that technology alone is insufficient to make knowledge sharing happen. Systems and platforms can facilitate knowledge sharing but are not likely to drive it. The systems you develop or acquire should be appropriate for your organizational context and aligned with the knowledge-sharing processes that your staff and partners are ready to use. Bhatt (2000) suggests that, while technology is certainly critical for a sound knowledge management strategy, its implementation requires far less effort than does behavior change and its accompanying support processes (figure 2.4).

Figure 2.4 The Distribution of Effort among the Three Components of Knowledge Management

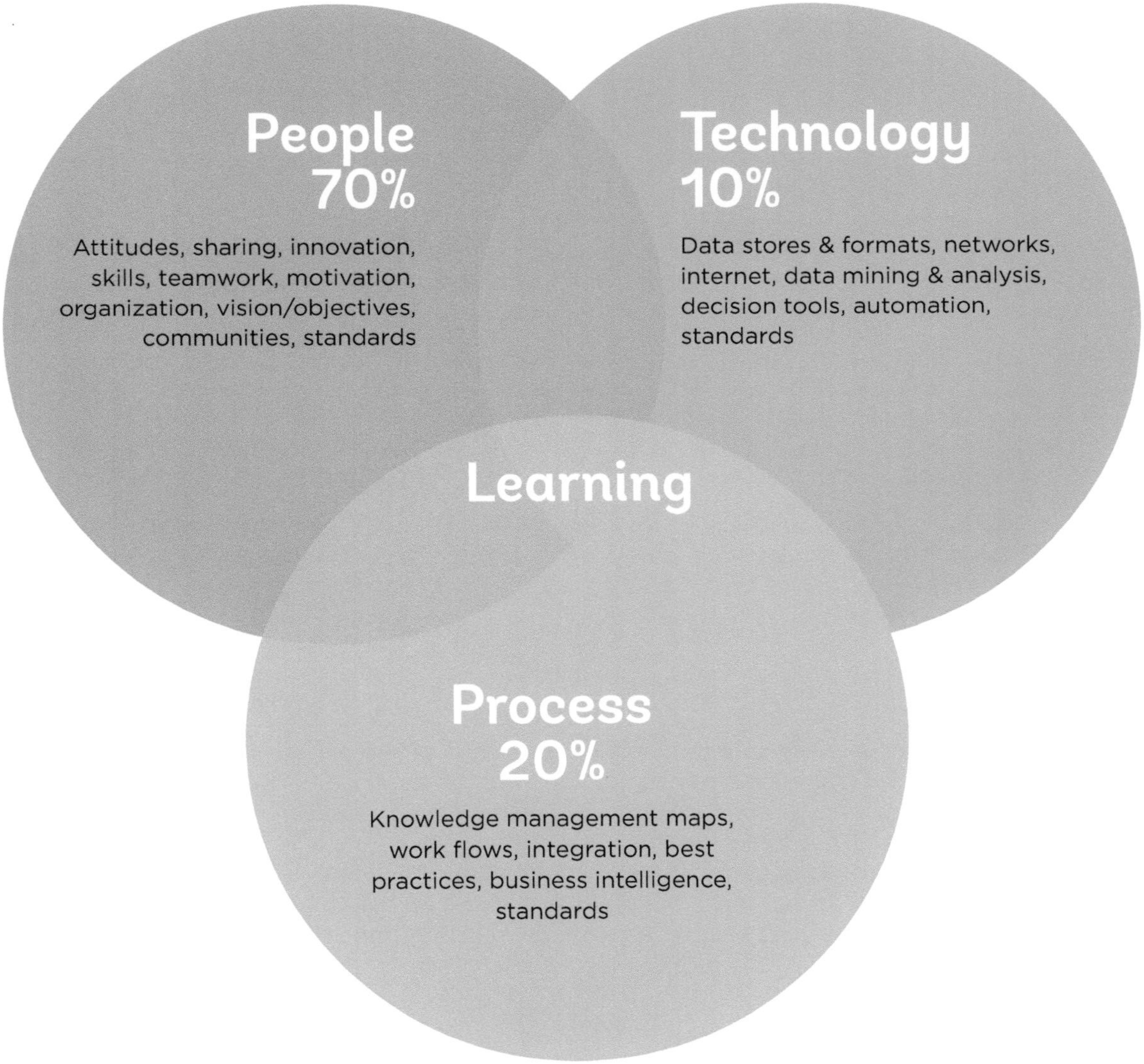

People 70%

Attitudes, sharing, innovation, skills, teamwork, motivation, organization, vision/objectives, communities, standards

Technology 10%

Data stores & formats, networks, internet, data mining & analysis, decision tools, automation, standards

Learning

Process 20%

Knowledge management maps, work flows, integration, best practices, business intelligence, standards

Source: Bhatt 2000

Knowledge Sharing in Action

Applying Information Technology to a Knowledge System for Disaster Management

Indonesia's Mobile "Disaster Management Solutions Finder"

The great challenge of emergency management agencies, such as Indonesia's National Disaster Management Authority (BNPB), is to apply knowledge and tested operational solutions not only to preparedness and reconstruction but also, in the heat of real time, to emergency response. Working with the World Bank to advance its mission, BNPB conceptualized and developed a tool, called the Disaster Management (DM) Solutions Finder, that allows access to the authority's online knowledge management system from smartphones and computers across Indonesia. The system works in both Bahasa Indonesia and English and over time can incorporate local dialects.

Users of the DM Solutions Finder can search previously captured knowledge assets for their applicability to current disaster management challenges. It includes a range of functions that BNPB staff members found essential, the ability to share knowledge assets with peers, full-text as well as categorical searches, and GPS location data and mapping. It also allows users to locate and contact experts who contributed to the system's repository of knowledge assets.

The web-based application works with all major mobile operating systems and requires little technical maintenance. As web access is not universally available, the solutions finder generates both a printed and offline version.

Knowledge sharing should add value and fit in seamlessly. Organizations offering blanket instructions for staff members to submit documents to a knowledge system often receive a great deal of redundant or low-quality information. Explain the objectives behind knowledge initiatives and provide training that will illuminate the benefits. Doing so will help ensure that staff members see the larger picture and that you don't make extra work for yourself sifting through unusable submissions.

People will need to see real value in any knowledge-sharing system. The effectiveness of such systems relies on the interaction between people, core work processes, and the technology that supports both. Good governance of knowledge sharing helps strike the right balance between these three components, thus making your IT investments more likely to have a valuable impact.

While an in-depth discussion of technology options goes beyond the scope of this guide, here are a few of the most common systems:

Intranet and extranet

An intranet is a web-based information network serving a single organization. It can be customized to offer information selectively by type of user (contractor, full-time employee, and so on) as well as by job function. Intranets can also be created for specific work units. Extranets are an extended version of an intranet that can encompass suppliers, customers, and partners located outside of the organization. Intranets and extranets increase the effectiveness of organizational information retrieval. They require maintenance, support, and curating to ensure ease of access and knowledge retrieval. Best practice assigns intranet and extranet maintenance to the IT function, which coordinates with departments through a knowledge-sharing task force.

Knowledge base

A knowledge base is a computer database technology used to store, administer, and access information in a systematic way. It typically includes a search engine and a web-based user interface.

Expertise locator

An expertise locator (or expert locator) identifies and provides convenient access to experts on a given subject. It usually features a profile page on each expert and a search engine. The profile pages, or white pages (see chapter 5, section 5.3.2), document the person's experience and specialty areas. The search engine allows quick identification of the right expert through either thematic browsing according to a predefined taxonomy or a keyword search. Expertise locators offer a powerful way to connect people unknown to each other who share a common interest or can help each other.

Use expertise locators to motivate staff contributions to the knowledge base. When linked to a pool of knowledge assets, such as documents, papers, and video files, expertise locators can be a great way to motivate staff to contribute to your organization's knowledge base. As knowledge assets created by an individual are added to his or her profile, they manifest that individual's growing expertise and can raise the value of the individual in the organization. Add rating functionality so peers can rate the usefulness of a given knowledge asset and thus further recognize the author.

Wiki

A wiki is a type of online knowledge base that contains a discussion page and an editing page for each knowledge topic plus a page of revision history (Wikipedia is perhaps the most famous Internet-based example). An organization-wide wiki system can allow staff members to share their insights and operational lessons learned in a systematic and continuous manner. The wiki is searchable and can be organized in line with operational core domains and support functions.

Learning management systems (LMS)

LMS are software applications for managing training and educational records and the delivery of e-learning courses and collaboration. Colleges and universities use LMS to deliver online courses and augment on-campus courses. Corporate training departments use LMS to deliver online training, as well as to automate record-keeping and employee registration.

Social media networks

Social networks can be very powerful knowledge-sharing tools. A well-targeted network can provide its members with access to highly relevant knowledge, connections, and advice. In a business setting, knowledge sharing via social networks allows companies to have a much closer relationship with customers and potential customers. Internet-based social networking has opened up a totally new way of managing customer relationships. (For more on social media networks, see chapter 7.)

Blogs

Blogs, short for "web logs," can be a great way to share knowledge. A blog is a frequently updated online diary or journal that can be run by one person (the blogger) or a group. Blogs can convey personal thoughts, passions, and stories while also being thematic. Depending on the software used, blog readers can comment on, rate, or further share any of the posted items.

Webinars

Webinars are meetings held in real time via the Internet. A webinar usually centers on a presentation and supports interactive discussion and question-and-answer segments. Participants can typically view the presenter and presentation slides as well as listen to the audio stream via their computers. Webinars are a cost-effective way to reach a large audience because participants do not have to relocate to take part in the session. Depending on the software used, webinars can be recorded for later use.

2.7   Conclusion

Knowledge sharing will not be effective if it is the work of only one person or department. It must be part of the job descriptions of all staff members at all levels of operation and support. Each individual and each organizational unit must have a clear understanding of roles and responsibilities assigned for capturing, storing, and sharing knowledge, and the appropriate skill mix for knowledge-sharing functions must be developed.

A knowledge-driven change management process should be spearheaded by senior management, but additional functions are needed to ensure sound planning and implementation. Although the use of outside experts and vendors can be helpful, the emphasis must be on developing an in-house culture in which knowledge capturing and sharing is a part of all activities. Likewise, technology can provide enormous help, but it is a means, not the end; the knowledge-sharing culture must provide the context for its use.

2.8   Checklist

Governance, Structures, and Systems	Yes
Are roles and responsibilities for knowledge and learning clearly defined in my organization?	
Do we have a working group that coordinates knowledge sharing?	
To what extent is knowledge and learning anchored in senior management?	
Are all departments actively involved in knowledge sharing?	
Is knowledge capturing and sharing part of each staff member's job description?	
Do we have the right skill mix for knowledge capturing and sharing?	
Is there clarity on which knowledge and learning functions should be situated internally versus externally?	
Do we have a user-friendly and accessible central knowledge repository (knowledge base, intranet)?	
Do we have IT systems that effectively connect people and ideas (expertise locator, intranet, blogs, etc.)?	
Do we have systems that facilitate collaboration (wikis, social media networks, etc.)?	
Do we have systems that facilitate learning (LMS, intranet, webinars, etc.)?	

3. BUDGETS AND FINANCING

Knowledge Sharing in Action

A Central Budget for Knowledge Management

Indonesia's National Disaster Management Authority

Recognizing the strategic importance of knowledge sharing, the management of Indonesia's National Disaster Management Authority (BNPB) budgeted central functions to support knowledge management. The functions included a data center (Pusdatin) and training center (Pusdiklat) for all learning and knowledge-sharing activities. The budget covers areas relevant to knowledge management and learning, including labor, equipment, and material costs as well as costs for national, regional, and local knowledge-sharing and learning events.

3.1 Why Is Financing Important?

A dedicated budget for knowledge and learning is an important indication that an organization takes knowledge sharing seriously. It signals that senior management is ready to invest in the knowledge and learning capabilities of its staff and the organization at large. Not allocating funds for knowledge and learning also sends a message to staff—that knowledge sharing may not be worth an investment. But without basic funding, good ideas and practices may quickly lose traction. Although it should always set aside some internal funding for the program, a knowledge-sharing organization can also complement its budget with external funding sources. This chapter provides a brief overview of the available options.

3.2 Developing a Budget

Knowledge sharing is a relatively low-cost function that nonetheless entails significant costs to cover planning and implementation.[1] An organization implementing

---

[1] According to an early 2000s study of five large U.S. corporations, the median number of employees participating in knowledge management was 42,000, the median annual cost of knowledge management per participant was $152, and the median reported gain, or "impact," was $357 (APQC 2003, as excerpted in APQC 2009).

a knowledge-sharing program will need to reallocate staff time or hire new staff to manage it, and it will have to provide funding to support technology, content development, event facilitation, travel, communications, and training. As Lipshitz, Friedman, and Popper (2007, 103) note, "For organizational learning to take hold, managers must make it an activity of central, strategic importance in the organization's agenda. One way of achieving this is instituting organizational learning mechanisms and appropriating the necessary resources for their proper operation."

A key element is the capacity to mobilize resources in an effective and sustainable way. Knowledge-sharing costs can be limited by integrating the smart use of technology in core operations. In most cases, the highest cost factor will remain staff time. Successful organizations recognize knowledge management and sharing as similar to staff training or information technology and thus include it as a normal part of a central overhead investment.

Costs for knowledge sharing may vary dramatically depending on a number of basic factors (figure 3.1):

» Size of the organization and knowledge-sharing objectives

» Number and geographic location of staff involved

» Staff capacities needed

» Infrastructure to be developed

» Choice of knowledge-sharing modalities and instruments

» Duration and frequency of the activities

Trade-offs must be weighed to determine the funding required for effective knowledge sharing. For example, face-to-face exchange is typically the most desirable form of collaboration, but the cost may be prohibitive for operations with limited resources.

Put your knowledge-sharing management and funding in a "big house." At the outset, a centrally funded knowledge-sharing budget may be most effectively managed within a support department such as communications, training, IT, or human resources or in an operational department with secure financing. As cross-departmental participation and ownership are critical to success, select whichever department provides the best chance for knowledgeable, holistic leadership, and organization-wide acceptance.

Figure 3.1 Factors Determining Knowledge-Sharing (KS) Costs

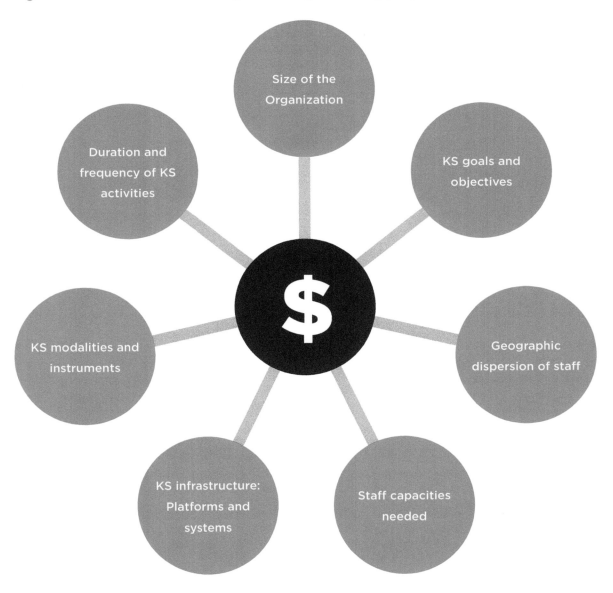

3.3   Sources of Financing

The central budget is often the initial source to pay for core knowledge-sharing costs. Each year's estimated costs for technical knowledge-management infrastructure and activities should be included in the annual central budgeting process. Central budget support is typically greater when an organization is embarking on its knowledge-sharing strategy. One advantage of central funding and coordination is that it reduces fragmented investments that may occur when a range of departments implement isolated knowledge-sharing initiatives with funds that were originally allocated to them for other purposes. Especially wasteful are uncoordinated investments in websites, databases, and other IT systems. However, expanded buy-in is signaled when department heads include in their part of the central budget a provision for knowledge sharing as part of "how we do our work."

Avoid allocating the majority of your knowledge-sharing budget to technology. Best-practice research indicates that technology allocations should be secondary to costs related to people and processes. Explore the viability of low-cost, commonly used technology options. If you overspend on a high-end IT platform but don't invest in staff participation, training, and support, the initiative may fail.

Here are a few examples of ways that organizations allocate funding across their departments to support knowledge sharing:

» An agency's core knowledge-management support team is funded from the HR budget, while the online platform is funded from the IT department. Community managers of thematic networks, and related activities such as exchange visits, are funded by individual departments.

» An intranet is created with central funding, while individual departments raise project funding and develop independent websites to support their collaboration needs.

» A central knowledge-sharing unit receives core funding for technology platforms and provides limited seed funding that initiates thematic communities of practice. Costs for staff participation, including webinars and travel, are covered by the relevant department.

While the use of departmental budgets may vary, central planning and oversight will be critical to avoid the wasteful duplication that can arise from uncoordinated knowledge-sharing activities across the organization.

A number of organizations are experimenting with a mix of financing sources, including government allocation, donor-supported funds, and multiyear programs. Nontraditional models of public-private partnerships, co-financing schemes, member fees, and revenue-generating knowledge-sharing activities are also high on the priority list for many institutions. To ensure that financing achieves sufficient scale and quality, organizations must develop a strong capacity for financial programming, execution, and accountability.

3.3.1   External cooperation funds and grants

Financing from national and international sources can often provide the catalyst for an organization to scale up its investment in knowledge sharing and IT infrastructure. The new capacities developed in this way—both in technical infrastructure and in specialized skills among staff members—enable the organization to support increased knowledge sharing at lower cost in the future. For example, a one-time grant from a private foundation may pay for an online collaboration platform that will function for several years.

3.3.2 Partnerships for financing

Knowledge sharing is commonly a collaborative endeavor involving peer organizations, universities, private sector companies, and networks. As your organization packages and shares its expertise, it opens the door to an expanding range of partnership opportunities (discussed in chapter 4). Partnerships are less likely to provide direct funding and more likely to bring matching funds, content, infrastructure, or personnel to a shared project. A corporate partner may provide technology, technical services, or lodging, while a university may provide meeting space, research assistance, or content-packaging support. These contributions reduce the demands on your internal budget and thus increase the funding available for other staff and activities.

3.3.3   Cost recovery

Service agreements or sponsorships from external agencies seeking knowledge-sharing products and services may be an attractive way to generate additional funding for a knowledge-sharing program. This financing model may not be possible in most public sector agencies; but in organizations whose legal framework permits it, a cost-recovery or fee-for-service approach may complement the institution's mission.

3.4   Conclusion

Ongoing financial support is essential to the success of knowledge sharing. A well-defined business model can deliver that support through a variety of mechanisms, including the central budget, development cooperation funds, and external partnerships. Agile responses to increasing external demands for knowledge sharing might be provided, to the extent allowed, by supplying knowledge services using cost-recovery strategies.

3.5   Checklist

Budgets and Financing	Yes
Do we have an allocation for knowledge sharing in the central budget?	
Is the budget aligned with our knowledge sharing strategy?	
Is staff time for knowledge sharing adequately factored into our budget calculations?	
Do we have a good understanding of the budget needed for knowledge-sharing infrastructure (platforms and systems)?	
Do we have a business model for knowledge sharing (for example, fee for service)?	
Do we need additional sources of financing for knowledge sharing?	

4. PARTNERSHIPS

Knowledge Sharing in Action

Partnering for Knowledge Capturing and Sharing

Uganda's Ministry of Agriculture, Animal Industry and Fisheries

The Ministry of Agriculture, Animal Industry and Fisheries (MAAIF) sees knowledge sharing as critical to its internal development and to improving its service delivery. But staff members, who are busy with existing programs and tasks, have too little time to fully execute the knowledge-sharing agenda. However, the mass communications department of Uganda's Makerere University has incorporated in its curriculum the World Bank's methodology for knowledge capturing and sharing. Senior management at MAAIF therefore entered into a strategic partnership with the university through which selected students and graduates of the communications program are invited to perform internships at MAAIF. While MAAIF expands its capacity to document and share its important experiences in its mission to improve agricultural productivity, the students get a practical introduction to knowledge and learning work in a national organization. Managers on both sides of the arrangement hope that it will eventually provide a sustained supply of qualified and trained knowledge workers for the ministry and Uganda's wider public sector.

4.1 Why Are Partnerships Important?

Partnerships are becoming necessary for any organization operating in increasingly complex environments (box 4.1). Some organizations choose to focus primarily on international partnerships to increase their exposure to good practice in their field. Another choice is to focus on domestic partnerships that enrich learning or allow a scaling-up of proven solutions. A third form of partnership concentrates on financing. Lastly partnerships can help with research and development, peer reviews, and knowledge capturing.

Box 4.1   Clarifying Terminology: Knowledge Partnerships

As defined by the Asian Development Bank (ADB 2011, ix), knowledge partnerships are associations and networks of individuals or organizations that share a purpose or goal and whose members contribute knowledge, experience, resources, and connections, and participate in two-way communications. They thrive when there is a strategic, structural, and cultural fit, when members embrace a collaborative process, behave as a coherent entity, and engage in joint action decision making.

Here are some key benefits of knowledge partnerships (figure 4.1):

» **Expanded skills base.** Partnerships allow your organization to access a greater variety and depth of expertise than it could ever develop in-house. Because partnerships provide such access in a regular and systematic way, they can enable your organization to multiply its force.

» **Capacity development.** Partnerships can enhance the technical performance and competence of your organization. Collaboration develops capacity at the individual level through staff learning and at the organizational level by expanding the ability to deliver high-quality services at greater scale.

» **Innovation.** Partnerships expose participants to new ideas, which in turn can spark innovative solutions. At a deeper level, partnerships nurture the trust and openness among participants that provides the most fertile ground for discovering and adapting new techniques, programs, and solutions.

» **Adaptation.** Partnerships enable organizations to adapt in a more agile way to rapidly evolving environments. Complex challenges, such as those generated by climate change, are not solved alone but rather through collaborating, learning, and adapting together with the expertise of others.

» **Financing.** Some partnerships are set up to increase financial support. In the development world, most partnerships are forged between national agencies and international donors. Domestic partnerships between, for example, state-level actors and NGOs are increasingly able to access national budgets.

Figure 4.1   Benefits of Knowledge-Sharing Partnerships

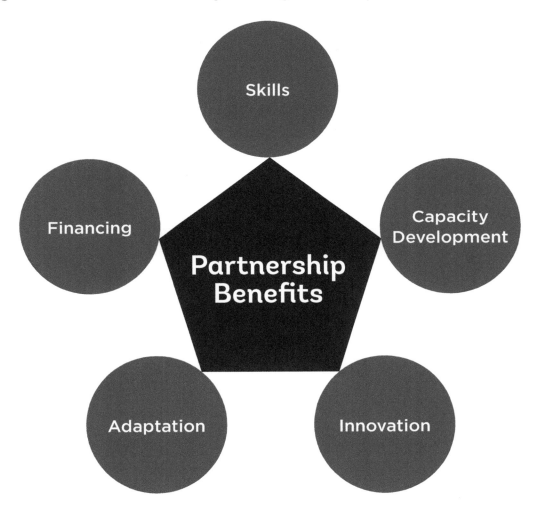

4.2   Informal and Formal Partnership Arrangements

Arrangements for partnerships range from informal collaboration to legal agreements.

A go-slow approach to formalizing partnerships is advisable. Consider the initial degree of collaboration and complexity required, and choose a less formal partnership arrangement until a more formal agreement is clearly needed. Resources invested at the outset to develop agreements and governance structures may be better used in exploring and learning from actual collaboration that can inform later formalization.

4.2.1   Informal partnerships

Informal partnerships often arise in response to specific needs. Staff members may collaborate with peers and other stakeholders outside the organization, for example, online in technical communities of practice or to create documents on a specific technical solution. Professional networks and conferences provide another opportunity for informal sharing of knowledge and experience.

Informal partnerships are especially valuable when ad hoc knowledge sharing is needed to address immediate challenges because their informal nature minimizes administrative delays and legal burdens. On the down side, however, they may receive less visibility within and beyond the organization, and senior management may therefore be less aware of them.

4.2.2   Formal partnerships

A formal partnership agreement, such as a memorandum of understanding (MoU), can offer several advantages over informal arrangements. First, it can strengthen the mandate by providing greater visibility to the collaboration, signaling to the respective staffs that engaging in knowledge sharing is desirable and encouraged. Second, the partnership document can better ensure that all participants understand the purpose and goals of the partnership and the knowledge-sharing activities to be undertaken to reach those goals. Third, for partnerships involving deliverables or financial transactions, a formal agreement can provide legal recourse in the event of noncompliance. Finally, organizations and their staff members involved in exchanges and secondments can be better protected under formal agreement.

While each partnership is different and caters to the respective needs of the organizations, an effective formal partnership generally has at least some of the following characteristics:

Shared concerns

- » Rooted in open discussion about needs, shared values, and goals
- » Aligned with the core mission and strategy of each organization

Mutually beneficial goals

- » Short- and long-term goals
- » Specific activities to attain goals
- » Alignment with goals and budgets of key departments and participating units

Activities integrated into cultures of the organizations

- » Alignment of activities and timelines with participating units
- » Frequent communication
- » Promotion of trust to share mistakes and challenge each other

Clear management process and structure

- » Assignment of a point person to monitor performance
- » Written descriptions of roles, responsibilities, and accountability measures
- » Training for all key personnel on the terms and potential benefits of the partnership
- » Written agreements such as memorandums of understanding (MoUs)

Support by senior management and participating departments

- » Alignment of business strategy with alliance strategy

Detailed communication plans

- » Regular communication among partners about intended and actual outcomes
- » External communication of partnership achievements
- » Structures and processes to capture and disseminate alliance knowledge

Clear definitions of success for all partners

- » Measures of progress established at the outset
- » Regular review of accomplishments, strengths, and weaknesses

4.3   Four Common Partnership Arrangements

4.3.1   Triangular partnerships

Triangular partnerships consist of alliances between, on the one hand, two or more agencies within developing countries and, on the other, international agencies or donors from advanced economies. In a triangular partnership the international agency supports and facilitates the knowledge-sharing activities between the developing country agencies. In addition international providers of assistance can help agencies in developing countries expand their knowledge-sharing capabilities, both as providers and receivers. Triangular cooperation has the potential to enable new types of partnerships between developing countries, sparking new relationships or deepening valuable exchanges within existing ones. The triangular framework for partnerships is being used worldwide to address complex global issues such as climate change and food security.

4.3.2   Networks

In an increasingly interconnected world, networks are important mechanisms for knowledge sharing. They can help coordinate the distribution of scarce and potentially worth sharing knowledge resources across multiple organizations. They can also accelerate innovation and adaptation of promising solutions among a broader range of members nationally and internationally. Country institutions need to be adept at initiating and sustaining purposeful networks—often with multiple partnerships embedded within their structure. Identifying and participating in existing networks, perhaps by building on relationships and exchange mechanisms that are already in place, can allow more resources to be devoted to actual knowledge exchange. The formation of a network can also be the natural evolution of a bilateral or triangular partnership, bringing in new partners that can enhance both the supply side and the demand side of knowledge sharing.

Cultivate the early involvement of senior management. The support of leaders will empower the staff to persevere in collaborations and knowledge exchanges that may not yield immediate visible returns.

4.3.3   Twinning arrangements and joint ventures

Twinning describes the pairing of one institution with a similar but usually more established or advanced institution for a mutually beneficial partnership. Twinning usually goes on for a multiyear period and can involve staff exchanges, secondments, expert visits, training, and technical assistance. Formal agreements that regulate financial and operational contributions can therefore be advisable.

In joint ventures, two organizations come together for a specific task or work collaboratively toward the same goal while retaining their separate organizational identities. They can last for varying lengths of time and usually end when the agreed-on task is completed. Joint ventures are governed by a formal agreement that specifies mutual responsibilities and goals.

4.3.4   Academic partnerships

Partnering with academic institutions can bring needed expertise and knowledge into the workplace, for example by providing a robust methodology for research or technical expertise for operational issues. In so-called "open education partnerships," agencies seeking to expand the dissemination of their technical knowledge may partner with academic institutions skilled in course development. For their part, universities and academics seek partners to get more direct access to the field to test theories or conduct research. Collaborative research partnerships bring together individual researchers or institutions to explore research questions of mutual interest and benefit. Partnerships can also focus on bringing in support for knowledge capture and sharing, which can be especially desirable in public sector institutions with limited staffing.

Depending on the exact arrangement, academic partnerships can offer a number of benefits:

» **Obtaining accessible, practical research.** Research can be packaged in a way that is more easily absorbed and applied—supportive of the MEL (monitoring, evaluation, and learning) agenda

» **Applying research.** Improve the likelihood of applying findings in actual operations

» **Observing in real time.** Embedded researchers observe the real-time chaos and improvisation of operations, rather than the retrospective coherence of a post hoc project evaluation

» **Expanding staff and education.** Student teams can help document and capture knowledge from operational experiences. Students can develop skills useful in the work force

» **Creating sustained relationships.** Single projects generate ongoing collaboration that links researchers and students to agency challenges

4.4   Conclusion

Partnerships are building blocks for sustained knowledge sharing between institutions. They can foster relationships for knowledge sharing in numerous ways, ranging from improvised approaches—with little structure beyond agreeing to share ideas either in person or through electronic means—to more deliberative, structured arrangements. They can be domestic or international in focus and can also create a financing arrangement.

The degree of formality needed varies with the degree of collaboration and the complexity of the context. Relatively informal partnerships may be governed under the terms of an exchange of letters and then evolve into longer-term, more involved collaboration that would require a more elaborate legal agreement.

4.5   Checklist

Partnerships	Yes
Do we systematically use partners to improve our current operations?	
Could our existing knowledge partnerships be expanded?	
Could local, national, or international partners help us deliver on our mandate more effectively?	
Are we ready to invest in mutually beneficial partnerships?	
Are we making use of academic partnerships?	
Could we outsource some knowledge-sharing tasks?	
Are we making systematic use of informal partnerships through our staff?	
Are we actively participating in knowledge networks?	

5. PRESERVING KNOWLEDGE: FROM IDENTIFYING TO FORMATTING

5.1 Why Is Preserving Knowledge Important and How Is It Done?

Now that we have reached the stage of actually creating knowledge resources, the benefits that organizations derive from capturing and preserving operational knowledge are worth reviewing. If knowledge is not preserved in some readily searchable and retrievable way, knowledge sharing has to happen directly between the knowledge provider and the knowledge seeker. Generally, direct transfer of knowledge is more effective than indirect transfer (Davenport and Prusak 1998) because it allows for deeper discussions and inquiry around details that may not have been captured in a document (figure 5.1). But the seeker and provider may not know each other or they may not be available at the same time. Documenting knowledge makes it available at all times, regardless of the availability of the experts, and offers powerful benefits:

- » Prevents the loss of experiential knowledge held by key staff members
- » Increases the speed and quality of decision making, especially by avoiding the repetition of mistakes
- » Builds unique resources for staff training programs
- » Builds unique resources for external knowledge sharing

Preserving knowledge consists broadly of four key steps, as discussed in this chapter and in more detail in the companion guide *Capturing Solutions for Learning and Scaling Up* (World Bank 2016): (1) identifying, (2) capturing, (3) validating, and (4) formatting. Chapter 6 discusses techniques of presenting knowledge assets for learning.

Although the four steps will not necessarily be executed sequentially (for example, validation should ideally happen throughout the process), all four should be built into the knowledge-management culture of your organization.

Before we get to these steps, however, we must define what kind of knowledge is worth the effort to capture.

Figure 5.1   Direct versus Indirect Transfer of Knowledge

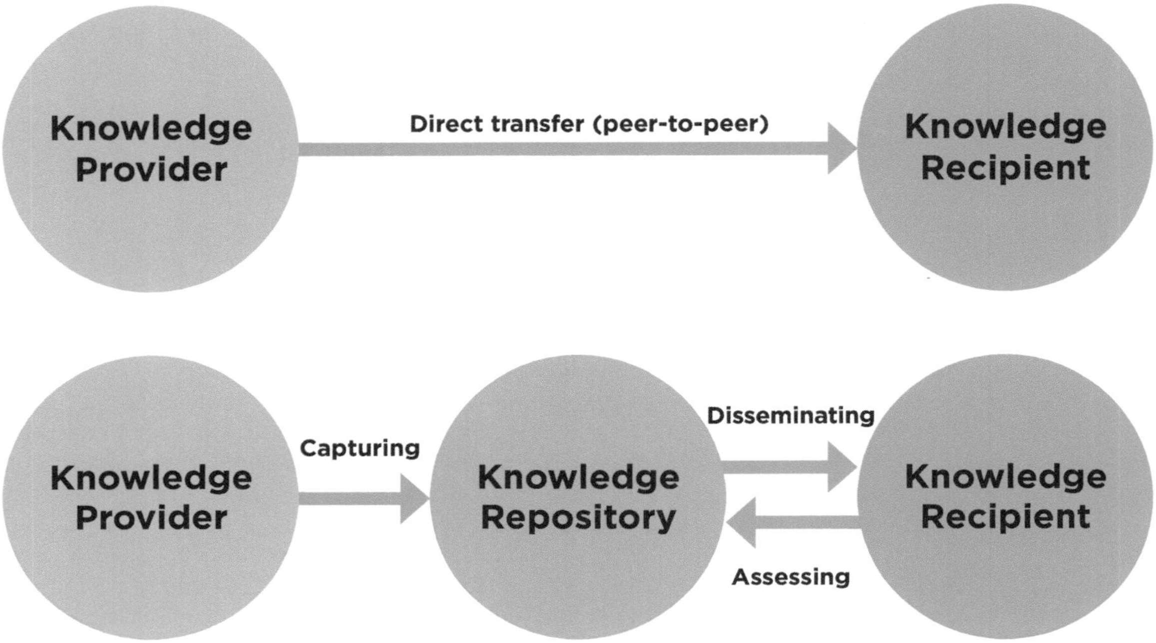

5.2   Defining Knowledge Worth Capturing

The right knowledge, available at the right time and in the right place, can be essential to overcoming barriers and improving decision making. But what is the right knowledge? Likely there is already a lot of knowledge held within your organization. This explicit knowledge is not the focus of this chapter, because it already exists in some form—books, reports, case studies, papers. We will concentrate our capturing efforts on the experiences of stakeholders in the organization. In other words, we aim to capture implicit or experiential knowledge.

Limited resources mean that organizations need to carefully evaluate their choices—an encyclopedic approach is impractical, not least because productivity would be drastically reduced if we tried to capture lessons from everything we were doing. Selectivity is critical because generally each captured knowledge asset needs maintenance and updating, and even then it often has only a limited life span. But the question remains, how do we choose?

An explicit set of criteria will help practitioners decide whether to capture a particular lesson learned from an experience or event. According to the American Productivity and Quality Center (APQC 2013), the most commonly used criteria include alignment of the potential knowledge asset with organizational strategy and the difficulty of replacing it if lost.

Figure 5.2   Criteria for Knowledge Worth Capturing

In a slightly more detailed set of criteria (figure 5.2), the potential knowledge resource should be:

1. Relevant—meets a demonstrable internal or external need

2. Narrowly focused

3. Worth sharing—artfully conveys insights or lessons learned

4. Easy to capture

5. Easy to validate

6. At risk of being lost

The first two criteria—*relevance* and *narrow focus*—are paramount. First, the potential asset must be deemed useful for some activity or it will not warrant documenting. Second, without a narrow focus, a knowledge asset is at risk of becoming a full-fledged case study—it becomes too broad, making the necessary information within it too difficult to find, thus violating the remaining criteria (a common problem).

The issue of focus applies to both the question addressed by the knowledge asset and the answer provided. The question addressed must be discrete and targeted; the broader the question, the less likely that the knowledge asset will provide a useful answer. The answer it provides must likewise be concrete, focused, and practical. If a range of answers emerge, try breaking up the knowledge asset into elements, each of which targets, and concisely answers, one specific question.

5.3   Systematically Assessing Your Organization's State of Knowledge

With these criteria in mind, organizations must still develop methods for systematically identifying existing and new knowledge. In this section we briefly describe some of the most common comprehensive practices for discovering knowledge that already resides in (or is missing from) the organization: the knowledge audit, white pages, knowledge gap analysis, social network analysis, peer-assisted learning, "premortem" project review, and challenge sessions. The next section examines methods of capturing new knowledge from ongoing operations.

5.3.1   Knowledge audit

A knowledge audit, sometimes also referred to as knowledge mapping, will often use some combination of methods to identify relevant knowledge ("content analysis") and the ways it is used ("process analysis"). The methods include online surveys, focus group discussions, and stakeholder interviews. The resulting document will show who "owns" the knowledge, how it was created, where it is located, how it flows among staff members and other key stakeholders, and how it is used.

5.3.2   White pages

Also known as profile pages, expertise locators, or capabilities catalogues, white pages help people identify colleagues within their organization who have the knowledge or experience they seek for a particular task. The catalogue, which can be assembled in part from the results of a knowledge audit, thus facilitates connections, knowledge creation, and new collaborations. Your organization's human resources function should keep the information current by encouraging periodic updates from staff members.

 Make sure that creation of knowledge assets is part of the white pages entries. Providing more visibility to authors of knowledge assets provides a strong incentive for staff members to contribute to the overall knowledge pool of the organization.

5.3.3   Knowledge gap analysis

In contrast to the knowledge audit, which looks at what is *available* in the organization, a knowledge gap analysis looks for what an organization is *missing*. The analysis compares current organizational competencies with required competencies, and the difference between the two represents the skills gap to be addressed. In the context of knowledge sharing, the analysis helps prioritize the areas in which knowledge needs to be identified and shared more broadly. A gap analysis can also be useful in identifying and developing new skills for emerging tasks.

Provide opportunities for staff members to identify knowledge that can meet their needs. People creating valuable knowledge may not realize that it could help colleagues in other areas of the organization, who in turn may not be aware of it. Look for ways that both staff needs and staff-created solutions can be publicized and linkages made—these can include FAQ systems, wikis, Q&A sessions, and dedicated newsletters.

5.3.4   Social network analysis

In the context of knowledge management, social network analysis creates a map of knowledge flows: From whom do people seek knowledge? With whom do they share it? In contrast to an organization chart, which shows formal relationships, a social network chart shows informal knowledge-sharing relationships. It allows managers to visualize and understand the many informal relationships and institutional structures that can either facilitate or impede knowledge creation and sharing. Storing the information drawn from a social network analysis can facilitate the monitoring and evaluation necessary to understand the outcomes of your investments (see chapter 8). A social network analysis can also provide important insights for the use of knowledge for "downstream" implementation by network members. It can reveal to what extent they have a vital interest in sharing and using the knowledge.

5.3.5   Peer-assisted learning

Peer-assisted learning is a simple, easy-to-implement process in which staff members organize a meeting or workshop to seek knowledge and insights from others in the organization. The objective is to cast a wide net for relevant but often undocumented experience and draw together a set of solutions from a diverse group of colleagues. The gathering also provides an opportunity to brainstorm new instructional content. Such meetings can also draw peers from external groups.

Depending on the scope of the task, the meeting can take as little as an hour. Include a facilitator who is not involved with the project at hand to provide a neutral, synthesizing perspective. Documenting the results of such meetings captures the procedural and substantive knowledge gained.

5.3.6   "Premortem" project review

In a medical setting, a postmortem allows health professionals to learn what caused a patient's death. In knowledge assessments, a premortem review is designed to fortify a project before launch by hypothesizing reasons it might fail and ways to avoid those outcomes.

The premortem imagines that the worst has already happened—that the project has failed spectacularly—and asks what went wrong. Participants independently write down every reason they can think of for the failure, including those that might normally go unmentioned in the interest of politeness; they then are encouraged to collectively imagine solutions to this array of hypothetical failures. The process can often reveal hitherto unrecognized insights, knowledge, and competencies.

5.3.7   Challenge sessions

Challenge sessions, sometimes called ideation sessions, are initiated typically when the organization or a team is facing a seemingly intractable problem and needs breakthrough. The challenge aspect is a two-way street. On the one hand, participants are given deliberately provocative statements about the situation. On the other, participants are meant to suspend hasty, conditioned judgment, tap into their own experiences, and generate solutions even though they may challenge conventional knowledge.

5.4   Systematically Capturing New Knowledge

We have defined the types of knowledge worthy of preservation and described various methods of discovering and portraying the organization's current state of knowledge; we now discuss how the organization can "capture" new knowledge being generated by ongoing operations.

The most valuable—because most worth sharing—form of knowledge is the "knowledge asset," a consistently structured and searchable digital product describing lessons learned. Capturing in the form of a knowledge asset is the critical action that permits the greatest scope for sharing internally and externally and over the long term. The methods you choose for capturing the content of the assets will depend on organizational policies and resources as well as on the preferences and skills of the capturer.

Knowledge assets need to be summarized and accurately described if they are to be made visible to other work groups and outside organizations. Titles, file names, and descriptions need to follow consistent formats and conventions so that searchers can accurately judge the content of an item from its description.

5.4.1 Knowledge capturing methods and strategies

The **interview** is the most frequently used of all knowledge elicitation activities. Interview questions and answers can be captured with the aid of a note taker or with a voice or video recorder. Interviews can be conducted in person as well as by telephone or videoconferencing. Interviews are also a method used by organizations to tap the otherwise undocumented know-how and wisdom of departing expert staff members.

Another method, the written **back-to-office report,** is used for following up attendance at an external business meeting or learning activity. By standardizing the format of the report, your organization can accumulate relevant data points for a richer knowledge product.

More collaborative methods of documentation are the focus group and the after-action review, usually conducted with a neutral facilitator. The focus group helps participants in a just-completed activity or project sort out their experiences and discover lessons learned. The after-action review focuses participants' attention on successes and failures of an operation or event *that was conducted by the organization*. It facilitates the assessment of organizational performance to support continuous improvement (see also chapter 8 for a discussion of its use in the monitoring of knowledge-sharing activities). See annex 5A for additional forms of knowledge documentation that often do not lend themselves as readily to conversion into knowledge assets.

Knowledge Sharing in Action

Systematically Capturing Local Experiences and Lessons Learned

Indonesia's National Disaster Management Authority

Indonesia has more than 400 local disaster management agencies, which coordinate their work with the National Disaster Management Authority (BNPB). The experiences of the local agencies constitute an "engine" generating a significant amount of knowledge as each disaster event is encountered and dealt with. To efficiently document and preserve that local knowledge, BNPB partnered with academic institutions with the intention of capturing lessons learned in the wake of each new event. Under the program, "capturing" teams—consisting mainly of students in, and recent graduates of, disaster management programs in Indonesian graduate schools—will be trained to conduct interviews with key stakeholders involved in disaster response activities. The interviews take place shortly after a disaster event (or even during it when possible) to ensure that recollections of circumstances, decisions, and results are fresh. The interviews are assembled and codified using standardized templates. The resulting knowledge assets consist of 2–4 pages of text that are enriched with video, photos, and other supporting materials. Through this effort BNPB is building a repository of native disaster management experiences that can inform responses to future events in a just-in-time manner. In addition, BNPB hopes to use the captured solutions as the basis for structured learning offerings to local government officials, disaster response teams, and other stakeholder groups.

The figure below illustrates how BNPB uses captured knowledge to provide just-in-time access to locally generated disaster management solutions and to enrich its training of disaster management practitioners.

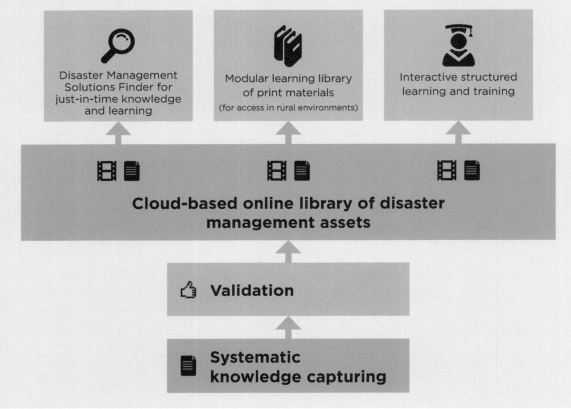

Every organization will need a knowledge-capturing strategy adapted to its specific context and business needs (see box 5.1 for examples).

» Small organizations with few staff members may choose to build a dedicated capturing team, with knowledge management and communications officers who frequently interview colleagues on important lessons learned. This is especially useful in organizations where staff readiness in terms of skills and incentives for capturing is low.

» Large organizations with geographically dispersed activities may need to complement internal teams with an external partner to help with knowledge capturing. Also, many organizations, especially in the private sector, provide incentives for staff members to continuously capture and share knowledge that is critical for business.

» Organizations with a strong knowledge-sharing culture can take advantage of decentralized capturing and sharing, a highly effective approach that requires strong systems for unified formatting of content and for rapid storage and sharing.

Box 5.1   Capturing Knowledge on Development Practices

Case studies

The Global Delivery Initiative (GDI) is an international collaboration to improve development outcomes by leveraging delivery know-how (http://www.worldbank.org/reference/GDI). The GDI has more than 30 partners, including government agencies, multilateral development banks, bilateral donors, universities, and nonprofit organizations. The GDI addresses the complex delivery problems and processes of development stakeholders through a variety of support measures. It also issues case studies, briefs, and notes. To support this knowledge-capturing approach, the GDI has developed a methodology for producing case studies, in which writers around the world have been trained.

Factsheets

To support documenting of experiences within the World Bank, the Science of Delivery Team has constructed an inventory of 292 tools and approaches in four pilot areas (the Governance, Health, and Water Global Practices, and the Climate Change Cross-cutting Solutions Area). Based on interviews with 110 task team leaders (TTLs) and sector experts, these tools and approaches can be used by TTLs to make better-informed decisions and increase the chances of success in interventions; the information is being disseminated via factsheets on the World Bank's website.

Solution-ing

The Blue Solutions and Panorama initiatives have jointly developed "solution-ing," a learning and innovation methodology for the management and equitable governance of marine and coastal resources. Solution-ing gathers, documents, shares, and recombines parts of successful approaches and makes them available online and through publications for reuse and replication (http://bluesolutions.info and http://panorama.solutions).

What Is a Knowledge Asset?

For a knowledge-sharing organization, we define a knowledge asset as a digital document or collection of media containing knowledge about a specific question or challenge. Typically short and learner-oriented, a knowledge asset presents key lessons learned from an operational experience and provides decision-making support for one particular challenge. The story it presents follows a standardized format—tracing the problem, actions, results, lessons, and recommendations—that makes the asset a self-contained lesson. It should be validated in a peer-review process and formatted with search metadata allowing it to be found within a larger knowledge repository.

5.4.2   The structure of the knowledge asset

A knowledge asset captures valuable experiential knowledge using a standardized template that focuses on a distinct challenge. Generally, the knowledge asset template should contain the following elements:

1.   Title

2.   Contextual information, including the challenge and its antecedent circumstances

3.   Actions taken to overcome the challenge

4.   Results of the actions

5.   Critical lessons learned from the experience

6.   Recommendations to peers who wish to apply the experience elsewhere

The more closely you adhere to this sequence in your capturing process, the easier it will be later on to turn the raw material you have recorded into a knowledge asset that others can learn from. See annex 5B to this chapter for more detail on each of these elements.

Once you have completed the development of the knowledge asset, go back to the title and check whether it still matches the scope of the final product. If the content of the asset has widened beyond what you set out to describe in the title, it may be best to split up the content into several more-specific assets, each with its own more-specific title.

Questions to help determine whether the title works:

- Will someone who has not yet gone through the knowledge asset know what it is about?

- Would the title also work for other stories? If so, it may be too generic.

5.5   Validating

Experiential knowledge is naturally subjective, influenced by underlying assumptions. For example, a government official who organizes a road closure for a construction project will likely have a different perspective on the closure than the commuter who uses that road daily. Hence, the inclusion of insights from many participants leads to a more comprehensive and valid knowledge asset. *Validating* is the process of ensuring that the knowledge asset is as complete, relevant, and accurate as possible.

Some form of quality control should be exercised throughout the process of creating the knowledge asset so that time is not wasted on a weak or redundant product. But ultimately, a defined process of validation must be applied at least to the finished product before it is allowed to be disseminated. Only high-quality assets should enter an organization's knowledge management system.

Perhaps the most critical issue in the validation process is what criteria to use. Organizations will need to carefully select and refine the criteria and determine their respective importance.[1] Besides confirming that the asset adheres to the requirements of the storyline and formatting as described above, include some of the criteria for deciding what knowledge is worth preserving (figure 5.2):

1. **Relevant.** Does the operational experience or lesson learned add to what is already known in this domain as good practice? Is it a valuable contribution to the operational practice of the organization?

2. **Focused.** Is the content self-contained (adequate context, relevant points of view)?

3. **Worth sharing.** Is the style and structure of the asset user-friendly and suitable for learning activities?

Finally, is there any risk created by the knowledge asset (reputational or legal)?

5.5.1   Validation structures

Validation structures range from self-review to review by external experts. We distinguish six ways to organize a validation function, ranging from informal to formal and internal to external, including two hybrid forms (figure 5.3).

Self-review (internal, informal)

In the lightest form of validation, the author decides whether the knowledge asset is acceptable. This is sometimes the approach taken by organizations that are closed communities of trusted experts or have a high degree of internal collaboration. Authors can consult colleagues and management, including people tasked with the development of knowledge assets. The advantage of self-review is that no other sources are needed and potential bottlenecks can be avoided. However, if the author is too closely involved with the experience, his or her objectivity may be compromised. Moreover, this approach is not likely to produce an expert assessment of the asset's user-friendliness and suitability for learning activities.

Crowd-sourced review (external, informal)

Crowd-sourced review—drawing on a larger group of users to critique and improve an asset—is becoming an increasingly popular validation process (Wikipedia being a familiar example). Collaborators may consist of internal staff members, or external users (such as clients or peers), or both. Typical validation processes within the organization are reporting inappropriate content, rating

---

[1]   See chapter 3 of *Capturing Solutions for Learning and Scaling Up* (World Bank 2016).

usefulness, offering comments, possibly even editing the content. The latter is often the case when wikis are used to store and publish operational experiences and lessons learned.

Management review (internal, formal)

In some cases, management may not be well qualified to review a very technical knowledge asset. However, because management is ultimately responsible for the knowledge assets, its involvement in validation will send an important signal that it values quality assurance in knowledge capturing.

External expert review (external, formal)

Experts from outside the organization are intended to bring objectivity that, in some cases, can provide a new perspective to the author. External experts can come from peer organizations, think tanks, universities, and research institutions active in the same field. They should also include knowledge management or learning experts to evaluate suitability for learning. Depending on the substance, experts can also be found in local communities or among beneficiary groups. Engaging external experts may require funding.

Figure 5.3 Six Validation Structures

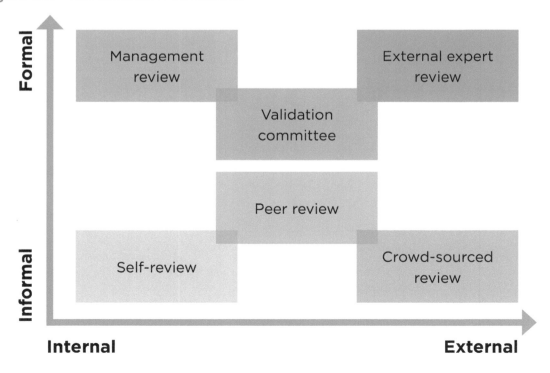

Validation committee (hybrid)

Validation by a designated group can provide a review where an assessment by management is not possible. Validation committees can consist of internal and external experts and knowledge management or learning experts.

Peer review (hybrid)

Colleagues give feedback on the correctness and value of the knowledge asset. Peer perspectives can include those of the experts involved in the experience, coauthors, clients, and disseminators of the knowledge asset. In some cases, involving reviewers who do not have a stake in the domain of the knowledge asset can be helpful. Peer review is cost-effective and provides quick feedback on the knowledge asset's usefulness in the operational context of the organization. In some organizational cultures in which negative comments are often interpreted as hostility, peer review may not be welcome.

5.5.2   Validation methods

The four most common methods for validating knowledge assets are (1) a real-life test, (2) examination by a group, (3) a check against validation criteria, and (4) verification with the initial experts or authors (figure 5.4). One or more of these methods can be employed in all of the validation structures just described, except self-review.

Putting the knowledge asset to the test

Although not often possible, directly applying the lessons contained in a knowledge asset to address a similar challenge may provide the most meaningful assessment of the asset's value and shareability.

Examination by stakeholders and peers

Stakeholders who can evaluate the asset for its applicability in their own context can provide important insights. Such reviews can occur in a variety of ways, including physical meetings and focus groups, individual interviews, and through online feedback such as voting, "liking," ranking, and recommending.

Checking against predetermined criteria

Organizations can define a number of evaluation criteria against which internal or external colleagues can assess the value of a knowledge asset.

Interviewing the authors

Interviews with the original experts or authors can help verify their expertise and the adequacy of the asset's conclusions and recommendations. Content experts, whether internal or external, can carry out these interviews best.

Figure 5.4 Four Validation Methods for Knowledge Assets

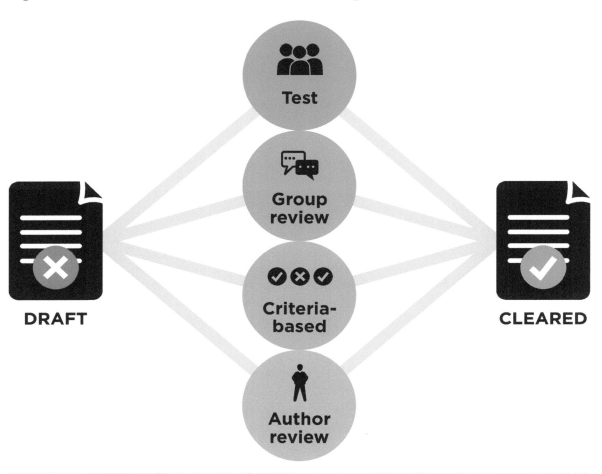

Validation is a dynamic process that continues throughout the life of a knowledge asset. Contexts may change and new insights may influence previously accepted conclusions. Some objects may become quickly outdated; others can be highly relevant for many years. Therefore, a schedule of dates for some form of regular reassessment should be applied to the asset so that it will be either reconfirmed, revised, or removed.

5.6   Formatting for Searchability and Accessibility

Traditional organizational knowledge is contained in lengthy reports and case studies that are often lodged in a traditional print library or in rarely accessed, difficult-to-navigate areas of an organization's intranet. Such documents and storage arrangements are usually not suitable when quick decisions are needed to move forward on a task. Time matters, and knowledge needs to be accessible and relevant to be useful. Professionals responsible for operations do not have the time to conduct extensive research or read those 100-page case studies to find the one bit of information they urgently need.

As noted in chapter 2, roles and resources must be devoted to formatting knowledge assets for searchability and accessibility. Doing so ensures that they adhere to a common standard of presentation and can be found by others, especially when dozens or hundreds of knowledge assets are eventually added to the digital knowledge library of your organization.

> » A common presentation standard provides a consistent and user-friendly appearance for all assets and allows the user to quickly and efficiently browse through them. This is especially relevant for assets containing several pieces, such as written material, video recordings, and images.

> » Including keywords, metadata, and other qualifying information to the assets adds to their searchability.

5.7   Conclusion

Systematically capturing practical experiences and knowledge helps organizations continually improve their mandated performance, retain critical know-how, and scale up successful solutions. The chapter provided criteria and mechanisms for identifying and capturing the important expertise and experience held by staff members and creating self-contained knowledge assets designed for relevance, searchability, and shareability. These assets help organizations accelerate decision making and avoid repeating mistakes. They are also unique and valuable resources for staff training programs and external knowledge sharing.

5.8   Checklist

Preserving Knowledge: Identifying, Capturing, and Validating Knowledge Assets	Yes
Do we know what knowledge resides in our organization?	
Do we have a place for knowledge as institutional memory?	
Are we systematically capturing our organization's relevant experiences?	
Is the knowledge we capture useful for more than reporting purposes?	
Do we have criteria that help us determine what to capture?	
Do we have the technical skills to capture knowledge?	
Are the knowledge assets we produce systematically validated to ensure high quality?	
Are knowledge assets formatted so they can be easily searched and found?	

ANNEX

5A. Additional Forms of Knowledge Documentation

1 Case studies

The case study is one of the most well-known knowledge products. Used widely in academic circles, case studies offer a method for sharing contextual knowledge that can help replicate lessons learned. They are based on actual events and offer an opportunity for analysis of a problem or scenario. Readers have the opportunity to develop and refine their analytical skills for solving similar problems that they may be facing.

2 Standardized lessons learned

Developing templates or formats to capture lessons learned from recent projects, activities, and operations makes institutional knowledge accessible to internal and external audiences. These can take a variety of formats, from traditional text-heavy documents to audio-visual products, such as guided interviews with practitioners or podcasts with a reference text. Lessons learned objects should be focused on addressing a concrete problem or challenge. They should also explain and describe how the problem was solved with concrete actions taken, the results achieved, and any lessons learned from the experience. These are most appropriate when they are case-based and offer concrete recommendations for action.

3 How-to guides

A how-to guide is intended to document organizational know-how on a specific process or sequence of activities involved in a core function of your organization. The guide should tap into the expertise of your staff members with the goal of accurately replicating a process to achieve the same results. How-to guides should be developed to share a particular practice or a unique approach that your organization is positioned to deliver. How-to guides are also made even more powerful when paired with experiential learning opportunities that connect knowledge seekers with the experts behind the how-to guide.

4 Concept notes

Concept notes offer the opportunity to share innovative practices, explore emerging trends, and shed light on topics that may offer "constructively disruptive" opportunities for your organization. A project concept note provides a preliminary description of a project and the theories and rationales that inform it. Approach concept notes as a venue to present trailblazing responses to challenges that require new or reconfigured approaches. Good practices that facilitate the development of concept notes include allowing time for staff to keep up to date with new trends and ideas, as well as creating spaces for cross-functional knowledge transfer.

5 Practice notes

Practice notes present an organization's position in relation to a specific functional area or practice area. These offer a more developed version of lessons learned papers as they include additional material to guide practitioners or decision makers, such as case studies, lists of experts and reference material for further research. A practice note should include a survey of practice from both within the organization as well as the latest research and academic literature developed externally. It is advisable to assemble a brain trust or a peer review team to provide input on the content as well on dissemination and presentation

6 Checklists

Checklists are a set of questions or procedural steps to be followed for operational accuracy, efficiency, consistency, and safety. Highly technical procedures are often complemented by checklists to reduce the margin of error. Their most prominent use is by pilots, who go through preflight safety and readiness reviews with the use of checklists. Hence, checklists can be a simple yet powerful way to capture knowledge on the critical steps that must be taken for a given task (see also Gawande 2009).

5B. The Structure of the Knowledge Asset

As noted in this chapter, the knowledge asset template should contain the following elements (figure 5B.1):

1. Title
2. Contextual information, including the challenge and its antecedent circumstances
3. Actions taken to overcome the challenge
4. Results of the actions
5. Critical lessons learned from the experience
6. Recommendations to peers who wish to apply the experience elsewhere

These elements are detailed here.

1 Title

The title should be explicit enough to convey the heart of the story and pique interest. A starting point is the "focus" discussed in section 5.2, that is, the question addressed by the knowledge asset. A good example would be, "How To Ensure Postdisaster Livelihoods by Cattle Evacuation through Upfront Engagement with Community Leaders"—it is clear and succinct while being detailed enough to convey the problem and solution being offered and thus to distinguish it from other knowledge assets. A more general and vague title, such as "Evacuating Cattle from Mount Sinabung," will not be nearly as helpful to practitioners who are grappling with a specific challenge and need concrete solutions.

Figure 5B.1 The Structure of the Knowledge-Asset Template

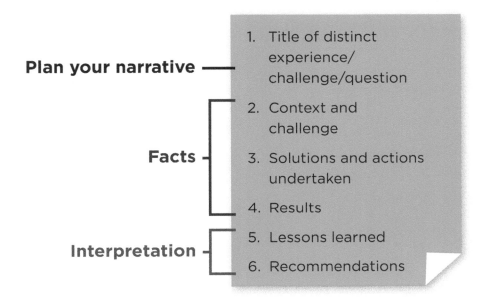

2 Context

Every challenge or question is rooted in its own circumstances that will likely affect its origins and potential solution paths. Background information can be critical in evaluating the relevance of an experience to another context.

Questions to solicit input on context:

» What is the challenge, problem, or event?

» What is its background, including causes and consequences and, if relevant, the sociopolitical and historical aspects?

» Where and when did the problem or event take place?

» Who was affected?

3 Actions taken

How did the actors deal with the challenge? Be sure to outline the options considered, solution paths, and the reasons for the chosen solution. Make sure you provide enough detail for others to fully understand and possibly apply the solution path to a new situation.

Questions to solicit input on actions taken:

» What actions were taken to overcome the challenge?

» Were other options considered?

» Who was involved in the activity and in what role?

» Were mistakes made, and if so, what were they?

» What barriers were encountered and how were they overcome?

4 Results

Results are important! Your audience will want to know the consequences of your actions. Create an outline showing to what extent the actions positively or negatively affected the challenge. As always, be concise but detailed in your description. If possible, quantify a certain result and measure it against a baseline. This information will provide credibility for the approach and will help others make informed choices on applying the solution elsewhere.

Questions to solicit input on results:

» What were the results of the actions taken?

» Are the results fully attributable to the actions taken or did other elements influence the result?

» Which activities led to which positive or negative results?

» Were there any additional positive or negative externalities worth mentioning?

» How did the various stakeholders react to the activities? Why?

5 Lessons learned

The lessons learned section is perhaps the most important part of the knowledge asset. Here you will provide a few major points that synthesize in simple terms the learning from the experience—what the expert would want recipients of the knowledge asset to remember. As in the other sections, specificity greatly enhances the value of the message: avoid generalities such as "Community involvement is important," "Adequate communication is critical," or "Timing is essential."

A good takeaway may consist of a summary statement followed by more detail in bullet points. For example, a summary statement need be no longer than the following:

> We built trust with the local community by engaging in advance with leaders and women's groups in two 3-hour facilitated focus group sessions. Each session brought together 25 to 40 participants and allowed us to collect expectations as well as address concerns at an early stage.

Questions to solicit input on lessons learned:

» What were the most important lessons learned from the experience?

» Why were they important?

» What would you do differently? What would you do the same?

» Whose involvement was important and why?

6 Recommendations

The purpose of the knowledge asset is to help others who may face similar challenges. The recommendations section is where experts present their conclusions about the potential transferability of the experience. Again, avoid generalities. For example, "Always involve all stakeholders early on" does not provide enough detail for action. Rather, in this case, state which stakeholders to involve, why, and when, and explain how to ensure their participation.

A summary statement followed by more detail in bullet points can be effective; for example:

> Successful resettlement of small communities in volcano-affected zones depends on preserving livelihoods, which may best be achieved by creating a cattle relocation plan. This plan should be developed with the local community early on to build strong buy-in. A sound plan contains the following elements: . . .

Questions to solicit input for recommendations:

- » What aspects of the experience seem most transferable to similar challenges?
- » What aspects seemed unique or less transferable?

6. USING KNOWLEDGE FOR LEARNING AND SCALING UP

Knowledge Sharing in Action

Knowledge into Learning: Building a Core Curriculum of Operational Skills

The Training Center of Indonesia's National Disaster Management Authority

Indonesia's National Disaster Management Authority (BNPB) is continuously orienting new employees and local disaster management officials while updating the skills and knowledge of existing staff and partners. To enlarge its capacity to teach the challenging real-life tasks of disaster management, BNPB invested in a state-of-the-art Training Center (Pusdiklat) focusing on skills development both for its staff and the staff of more than 400 affiliated local agencies spread across the country, which are typically at the front line of disaster management operations. The agency also acquired virtual tools, such as videoconference facilities in 20 selected provinces linked to mobile units through satellite connectivity.

Initially, the Training Center used localized versions of training modules from other disaster management agencies around the world. To improve the relevance of its materials, the Training Center began systematically and continuously modifying their modules, incorporating local disaster management experiences and turning them into high-quality knowledge assets and distance learning modules. It then deployed the assets in an interactive and participatory instructional design including role playing, simulations, debriefings, and group discussions.

6.1 Why Be Strategic about Using Knowledge Assets?

Knowledge assets must be readily searchable and available to serve immediate operational needs, but they are also a valuable resource for training new and existing staff members and for building knowledge-sharing relationships with other organizations. In chapter 5 we covered ways to create knowledge assets. We now confront the next question: what is the best way to embed knowledge assets in a training, orientation, or other learning offering? The answers will be derived from the answers to another question: how do adults learn?

Many books have been written on learning theory, and it is beyond the scope of this guide to introduce the plethora of approaches. But some core principles and tips can help increase the success of teaching, be it in a traditional classroom or workshop setting, an online learning environment, or on-the-job training.

Through the concept of "the learning design cycle," we briefly survey the methods by which individuals engage with knowledge assets ("learning") to inform the strategies for presenting those assets in a learning offering.

6.2   Embedding Knowledge Assets in Learning Offerings: The Learning Design Cycle

To create a successful training, you can use the "learning design cycle," a stylized sequence of steps intended to illustrate the process of designing an impactful learning experience (see figure 6.1).

Each of the steps in the learning design cycle are discussed below.

6.2.1   Clarify the goal

Laying a solid foundation for learning requires a clear understanding of the overall goal of the learners—What problem are they trying to address? What would success look like? For example, a ministry of agriculture that aims to stimulate greater agricultural productivity must have certain capabilities to devise and implement the needed policies. Is the ministry seeking tools and knowledge to improve those capabilities? Which ones in particular? How would they know if the learning succeeded? Clarifying the answers to such questions is essential to the success of the learning offering. The next step continues the clarification process by identifying the exact nature of the audience and its learning needs.

6.2.2   Define the audience and its learning objectives

No matter how limited or extensive the learning product, its design requires a clear understanding of the target audience. Using a "5W-1H" questionnaire can help determine critical characteristics of the audience (figure 6.2):

The "What" question focuses on the *learning objectives*, which are the value proposition of a learning product. They are the promises that a learner invests in and against which the offering will be evaluated. Learning objectives can be grouped into five categories that correspond to five levels of learning: remembering, understanding, applying or analyzing, evaluating, and creating.

Figure 6.1 The Learning Design Cycle

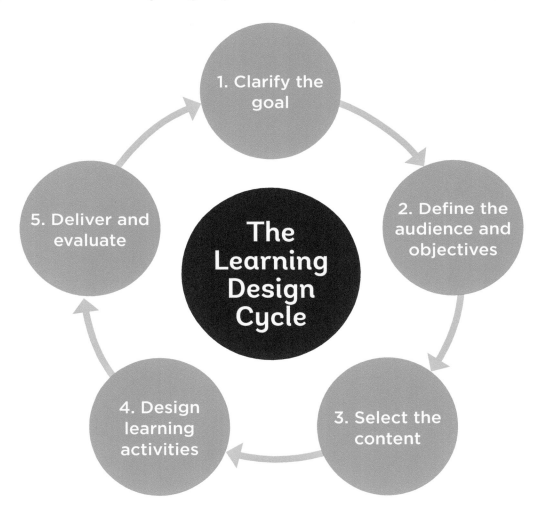

An additional helpful concept comes from Malcolm Knowles' 1970s work in adult learning theory (Knowles, Holton, and Swanson 2012). He introduced a model based on four principles of adult learning: involvement, experience, relevance, and problem orientation. Other work (Craig 1996, 253–64) added additional principles (figure 6.3):

Readiness. Adults become ready for a learning experience when they have a concrete need to know something.

Motivation. Adults are motivated by both intrinsic and extrinsic incentives. It is important to fully understand why adults are motivated to participate in a learning offering.

Figure 6.2   The 5W-1H Questionnaire

Who	Who needs to be targeted and at what level of the organization?
What	What is their background and what are their specific learning needs?
Where	Where are they located?
When	When are they available and when do they need to have the knowledge?
Why	Why are they interested, and why should they learn this material?
How	How large is the audience and how can it best be reached?

Figure 6.3 Principles of Adult Learning

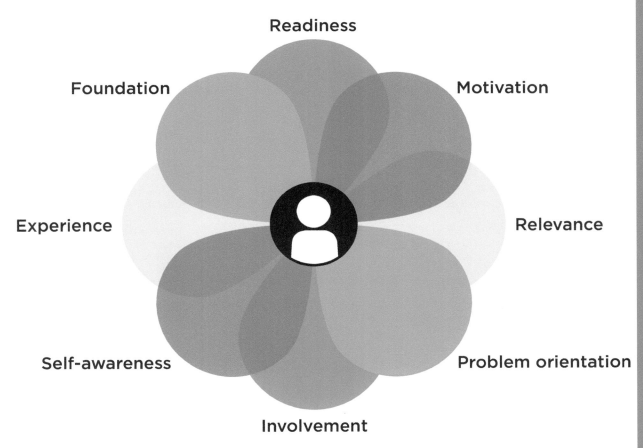

Source: Adapted from Craig (1996) and
Knowles, Holton, and Swanson (2012)

Relevance. Adults have a certain need to know that stems from a particular problem they have to solve. Activities should therefore be based on real work experiences that help to overcome the challenge.

Problem orientation. Adults enter into a learning experience with a problem orientation, not a content orientation. Learning activities should focus on "doing" something instead of simply "knowing" it.

Involvement. Adults should be involved in the planning and evaluation of their instruction.

Self-awareness. Adults have a need to be self-directing. Learning offerings should therefore be presented with various options.

Experience. Experience, including mistakes, provides the basis for the learning activities.

Foundation. Adults have a greater volume of practical experience than younger learners, and learning activities should build on this experience.

Know who your learning offerings are for and how they will be used.
Consider engaging your end users early in the development process to gain their perspective on the types of learning offerings best suited to their needs. The result could be a suite of similar offerings based on a core principle with variations to better serve differing types of users.

Systematically formulate the learning objectives with an action verb describing what the learner will be able to do after having completed the learning offering. Here is a common formula:

After the *[training, session, chapter, etc.],*
you will be able to *[action verb: understand, apply, etc.]*
[substance: a task, system, etc.].

For example, a learning objective for this chapter could be as follows:

After reading chapter 6, you will be able to apply the six-step learning design cycle to design high-impact learning products.

6.2.3   Select and format the content

Learning is a result of access to content and engaging with the content through reflection and application. Content can come from many sources, but the knowledge assets covered in chapter 5 are already tailored to your operations. Think through which knowledge assets would be relevant for learning offerings and assemble or package them for use in learning activities. Good learning products engage us by being

- » Succinct and to the point
- » Interesting if not downright intriguing
- » Designed to evoke reflection and provoke reaction
- » Application oriented
- » Well sequenced
- » Built to reach a set of specific learning objectives
- » Keyed to a particular audience

» Professional looking

» Easy to understand

» Produced in a language comfortable for the audience

Achieving these characteristics is not easy. A few guiding principles can help you accomplish this difficult task:

» Identify the "need to know" information.

» Identify the "nice to know" information and continuously ask if it is useful and relevant.

» Be problem- and solution-oriented.

» Keep the audience and the learning objectives in mind at all times.

» Present material in a variety of ways, for example by adding audiovisual components. Sometimes adding just a picture can do wonders to enrich a message.

Here are tools and modalities commonly used for presenting content.

Tools

Tools can be divided into four groups (see table 6.1):

» Print and presentation

» Audio-visual

» Direct interaction

» Distance learning

Table 6.1 Learning Tools and Their Media

Print/Presentation	Audio-Visual	Facilitation Techniques	Distance Learning
Brochure	Video clip	Flipcharts	E-discussion forum
Workbook	Audio clip or podcast	Post-It notes	E-mail
Checklist	Multimedia presentation	Polling	Blog
PowerPoint presentation	Simulation/model		Wiki
Spreadsheet	Game		E-survey
Case document	Radio		Live collaboration platforms
Facilitation guideline	Audio or video live stream		Social networking platforms
Newsletter			Videoconferencing and web-based conferencing tools

For distance learning, choose between "synchronous" and "asynchronous" tools. Is the audience local, or at least contained within two neighboring time zones? Then choose videoconferencing and webinars, which are live and thus synchronous. For an audience spread across wider time differences, e-learning tools and other asynchronous methods will work better, as they do not depend on simultaneous participation.

Delivery modalities

It is useful to think in terms of four major delivery modalities:

- » Face-to-face
- » E-learning
- » Videoconferencing
- » Mass media (print, radio, TV, Internet, and mobile phones)

The chosen delivery modality will be influenced by the constraints identified in the second step of the learning cycle (define the audience and its learning objectives, section 6.2.2), such as geography, knowledge level of the audience, availability, and financing.

Face-to-face

Face-to-face or classroom-based learning is the modality of choice for in-depth peer learning and group situations in which trust building is a major objective. Face-to-face learning offerings tend to be more expensive than technology-facilitated offerings because participation is limited and may include travel expenses.

E-learning

E-learning is becoming increasingly popular because it allows for individual pacing and accommodates thousands of learners widely dispersed across time zones or geographic distance. E-learning may be less effective when trust building and collaborative leadership building are among the objectives.

Videoconferencing

Like e-learning, videoconferencing is part of the distance-learning family of delivery modes. But unlike e-learning, it brings together geographically dispersed learners in real time in two or more connected locations. Videoconferencing can be used for presentations, with participants connected only in listening mode. However, it is best to use it for live interaction. Advances in high-bandwidth connectivity and online conferencing tools have improved the affordability of this modality.

Mass media

The Internet has become perhaps the premier medium of mass communication, at least for younger generations. However, even when not delivered via the Internet, print and broadcast media—books, case studies, reports, journals, newspapers, documentaries, and even TV or radio soap operas—continue to be important channels for learning.

Teachers often mix delivery modes into blended offerings. A common approach is to cover basic material and background knowledge through e-learning and then use face-to-face modes such as workshops and classroom-based learning for discussion, trust building, and social interaction.

6.2.4   Design learning activities

The content created in the preceding step is deployed through learning activities. A common belief of many presenters is that listening to a presentation results in learning. In part, yes. But research and modern learning theory indicate that the issue is complicated by variations in personal styles of learning (Kolb 1984, 5–10). As learners, individuals can be broadly grouped into four types (figure 6.4):

1. **Accommodators** learn best through experience and personal involvement. They enjoy case studies, skills practicing, group discussions, and simulations.

2. **Divergers** learn best through observation and reflection. They enjoy lectures with extensive time for reflection, expert interpretation, and room for imagination. Divergers are good listeners and are interested in people and their emotions. They also tend to be more imaginative.

3. **Assimilators** learn best through theory and concepts. They prefer working with abstract models rather than application and interpersonal experience.

4. **Convergers** are interested in practical application of concepts and ideas. They create new solutions and tend to prefer technical tasks over interpersonal challenges. Convergers enjoy field work, the application of practical skills, and working in labs or through self-directed learning.

The key goal of this step of the learning design cycle is to incorporate all four of these learning styles in the educational program, allowing the learner to (1) interact with peers, (2) reflect on the content and its relevance to a new setting, (3) conceptualize, and (4) formulate concrete action toward adoption, adaption, application, and replication of knowledge and experiences. Creating such programs is an art practiced by good instructional designers and facilitators. While presentations have their place as a way to deliver *information*, there is no deep learning without real engagement.

We distinguish between three main types of delivery methods: (1) mass, (2) individualized, and (3) group oriented. The method you use will depend on the context, the size and type of the audience, and the constraints within which the learning offering will be rolled out. Generally, you should combine delivery methods so as to cater to individuals' different learning styles and create a richer learning experience (table 6.2).

Figure 6.4   Learning Styles

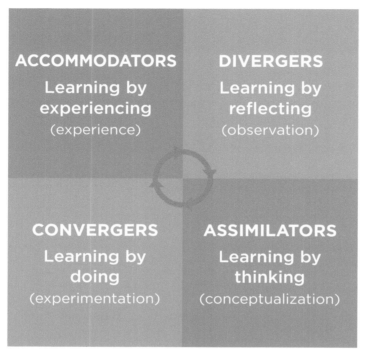

Source: Adapted from Kolb (1984)

Table 6.2   Overview of Delivery Methods

Mass Instruction	Individualized	Group Oriented
Lectures and similar expository techniques	Paper-based self-study materials	Class discussions, seminars, group tutorials
Film and video presentations	Self-instruction via mediated materials	Group projects
Educational broadcasts	Directed study of material in textbooks	Buzz sessions and similar small-group activities
	Computer-based learning and multimedia	Participatory exercises such as games, simulations, case studies
	Individual assignments, projects	Mediated feedback/discussion sessions

6.2.5   Deliver and evaluate

Learning activities need good logistical support: the room setup deserves careful attention, and the IT arrangements and audio-visual hookup should always be tested before sessions begin. Above all, however, learning activities need a skilled leader or facilitator who understands and applies a few key principles. Adhering to the following guidelines will very likely result in a successful learning experience:

» **Set some ground rules:** Have the group agree on some ground rules before starting the learning event. Muting cell phones, as well as listening to each other's contributions, are examples of ground rules all participants should agree to.

» **Clarify expectations:** Before starting, capture participants' expectations. Depending on the expressed needs, adjust the agenda and activities to meet your audience's expectations.

» **Be neutral:** Facilitation should be provided from a neutral position that helps the participants advance through the activities.

» **Be clear:** Clarity about the activities and how they are conducted is critical. Make sure all participants understand how to engage with the material. Once the procedures are set out, they should be upheld but not too rigidly.

» **Keep the time:** Time keeping is always a challenge as agendas tend to be over-packed. Make sure you balance the participant's needs to contribute and reflect with your need to cover all content. In most cases, less is more—it is more important for participants to remember 75% of the key takeaways than to remember only bits and pieces from 100% of the entire content covered.

» **Allow time for reflection:** Learning happens through reflection on the substance. A good facilitator allows the participants enough time to engage around the content. Allow small groups the opportunity to share their activity experiences with the larger group.

» **Adapt activities to participants' expectations:** As each group is different, a high level of flexibility is important for optimal learning.

» **Keep participants' interest:** A balance between cooperative and competitive activities usually works well for most audiences.

» **Listen and foster participation by all learners:** A facilitator is above all a good listener. Most of the learning will actually be generated by the participants. Listen carefully in order to summarize key points and draw links between contributions. Also provide the time and encouragement for everyone to speak up—especially important for more introverted participants and for the overall quality of the learning session.[1]

» **Focus on the learning:** In each group, the facilitator will need to balance individual learning needs with those of the group at large. Additional tasks can be provided for some participants.

» **Make time for future planning:** Provide time for the participants to summarize their key takeaways and how they plan to use them in their work.

After its delivery, the learning experience must be evaluated to determine whether it met its goals and offers any lessons for future programs. Evaluation is best conducted within a system that monitors and evaluates your organization's entire knowledge-sharing program—the subject of chapter 8.

This completes the learning cycle. Remember, the learning cycle is not a static framework but a flexible and evolving process that you build through evaluation and iteration.

---

[1]   According to a *New York Times* report, a study by Google found that one of the attributes of good work groups that distinguished them from teams that faltered was that "members spoke in roughly the same proportion" over the course of their work. Said the lead author of the study, "As long as everyone got a chance to talk, the team did well. But if only one person or a small group spoke all the time, the collective intelligence declined" (Charles Duhigg, "What Google Learned from Its Quest to Build the Perfect Team," *New York Times Magazine*, February 28, 2016, http://www.nytimes.com/2016/02/28/magazine/what-google-learned-from-its-quest-to-build-the-perfect-team.html).

Knowledge Sharing in Action

Managing Knowledge Assets

Lagos Metropolitan Area Transport Authority, Nigeria

The expertise of the Lagos Metropolitan Area Transport Authority (LAMATA) must be preserved and continuously made available to staff members to equip them with the latest knowledge from actual operational experiences. LAMATA systematically captures operational experiences and lessons learned. It packages them as knowledge assets, and knowledge-management officers from various departments upload them to a dedicated space on the organization's intranet. Staff members can search with key words or employ more granular criteria, including department of the author, project name, date of the incident or when it was recorded, and stakeholder group involved.

Learning should be relevant and fun! When designing learning offerings, keep the audience engaged. Put yourself in the shoes of the learner. Would you rather sit through hours of lectures or engage with your peers in a problem-solving exercise that helps you overcome a challenge in your work? Active engagement with peers and experts, contributing to the development of practical solutions, and doing so in a fun and interactive way also builds strong ownership because the learner has helped discover and develop the lessons ultimately learned.

6.3   Embedding Learning in the Activities and Processes of the Organization

Your selection of knowledge assets and learning offerings should take into consideration your organization's capacities and resource constraints. Each offering needs to clearly add value to your organization and not be seen as a burden. To realize the value and minimize any burden, it should have a production plan that includes a timetable, clear roles and responsibilities for execution, and realistic cost estimates.

The first steps in producing a knowledge offering—understanding your target audience and their objectives—will also help you identify the relevant departments or experts who can help lead or fund the design and development process. For example, the responsibility for learning offerings intended to improve administrative or technical capacities may reside in your organization's human resource department with support from experts who can share their expertise.

Other products and offerings may support your organization's outreach and partnering efforts. These may require that your communications department lead the effort or that coordination between departments be established to launch these activities.

6.4   Conclusion

Using the full potential of knowledge assets means actively deploying them in learning offerings—orientations, trainings, knowledge-sharing events with partner organizations, and so on. The question is, how best to do that? What does learning theory and research tell us that will help us make the best use of the knowledge assets in the teaching and mutual knowledge-sharing context?

The overarching principles are to know the audience, its objectives, and their constraints; and to present the knowledge asset in an environment that requires the participation of the learners—the more active their involvement, the more memorable the learning.

Capturing and sharing knowledge is an art; its practice requires continual assessment and adjustment if it is to meet its goals. As offerings become more effective, their success will help improve service delivery and in turn further strengthen the role of knowledge sharing and learning in your organization.

6.5   Checklist

Using Knowledge for Learning and Scaling Up	Yes
Do we have a good understanding of who needs to be learning what in our organization and among our partners?	
Are our learning offerings tailored to the needs of our management and staff?	
Are we using directly relevant knowledge and our own experiences in our learning offerings instead of relying solely on generic literature and concepts?	
Are our learning products succinct, accessible, intriguing, problem-oriented, practical, and well sequenced?	
Are we using the appropriate delivery modalities for our learning offerings?	
Are our learning offerings accommodating different learning styles?	
Are our learning offerings "learner-centric" instead of "teacher-centric"?	

7. THE HOW-TO OF KNOWLEDGE SHARING

Knowledge Sharing in Action

Creating a Knowledge-Sharing Culture through Storytelling

DANE, Colombia's National Administrative Department of Statistics

As a leading statistical agency with a strong mandate for international cooperation, Colombia's National Administrative Department of Statistics (DANE) continuously seeks to improve its performance. But as in any organization, the most experienced staff eventually move on or retire. To avoid losing the vast know-how of these staff members, DANE organizes events in which their knowledge is shared with a wide internal audience. Interestingly, the departing staff do not make the presentation. Rather, in advance of the event, they make a proper handover of their expertise to their colleagues, who in turn use the event to present the critical aspects of their new roles. The departing staff are in the audience, making sure that the content is correct and that their successors are fully equipped to excel in their new jobs.

The sessions are popular. Staff members throughout DANE strive to enlist as presenters, and the recognition they receive from peers and managers in attendance reinforces DANE's burgeoning culture for internal knowledge sharing.

Rather than reinventing the wheel or creating another layer of documentation, DANE repurposed their existing knowledge for better results. This low-cost measure engages the staff, helps to build institutional memory, and demonstrates to management the value of knowledge sharing.

7.1   Why Is Systematic Knowledge Sharing Important?

Organizations engage in knowledge sharing for three principal reasons:

1. Become better at what they do by producing higher-quality output or services and overcoming obstacles faster

2. Make themselves more independent from select staff members by equipping more employees with critical knowledge

3. Replicate and scale up successes and avoid repeating failures

Knowledge sharing can improve all levels of an organization's operation. *Internally,* it can help develop collaboration and innovation among staff members and avoid the loss of mission-critical know-how. *Domestically,* it can equip local partners with critical knowledge and solutions, including for policy implementation. *Internationally,* it can inspire new solutions and development pathways that stimulate change and reforms. This chapter provides a brief overview of common ways to practice knowledge sharing at those levels and discusses some ways to overcome obstacles.

7.2   Knowledge Sharing Starts with Listening

Knowledge-sharing engagements require preparation, and the single most important act of preparation is *listening before sharing*. Preparatory listening is required regardless of whether the sharing will be internal or with external stakeholders. It takes on even greater significance for international knowledge exchanges, be they South-South, South-North, or North-North interactions. The listening can be a water-cooler conversation, a phone call, or even a preliminary meeting or videoconference. Knowing the audience and its distinct challenges by *listening before sharing* will be essential for any knowledge sharing to succeed.

Become part of an active knowledge economy in your organization. Quite often an organization's right hand does not know what its left hand is doing. According to a researcher (quoted in Lipshitz, Friedman, and Popper 2007, 113):

> The biggest barrier to transfer [of knowledge] was ignorance . . . At most companies, particularly large ones, neither the "source" nor the "recipient" knew someone else had knowledge they required or would be interested in knowledge they had. The most common response from employees was either "I did not know that you needed this" or "I did not know that you had it."

> By offering your own know-how in discussions with peers and being willing to ask for advice, you can contribute to the knowledge economy in your organization.

7.3 Practices that Encourage an Internal Knowledge-Sharing Culture

Davenport and Prusak (1998, 88) provide an interesting answer to how organizations can transfer knowledge effectively. "The short answer, and the best one, is: hire smart people and let them talk to one another. Unfortunately, the second part of this advice is the more difficult to put into practice."

Organizations learn at three levels (figure 7.1): individually, through its employees; collectively, through its teams; and institutionally, at the organizational level (DuBrin 2005, 346).

» At the individual level, learning takes place through intuition and interpretation of actions and events in the organization. These can trigger further action, such as course-correcting measures in case of nonperformance.

» At the group or team level, learning has an integrative dimension. For example, joint learning can result in a common understanding among team members about a work-related challenge. Dialogue and collective thinking, including collaborations between team members, can generate a coordinated set of actions.

» At the organizational level, learning leads to institutionalization of actions. If deemed successful, the one-time actions developed at the group level can be turned into regular, standardized mechanisms through which the organization addresses reoccurring challenges. At this level, learning becomes fully embedded in the organization.

Figure 7.1   How Organizations Learn

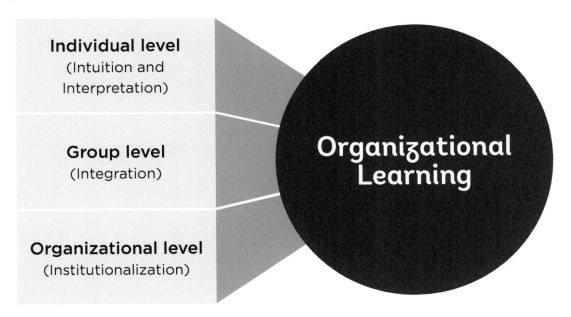

Source: Crossan, Lane, and White (1999, 525)

Figure 7.2 Examples of Internal Knowledge-Sharing (KS) Activities

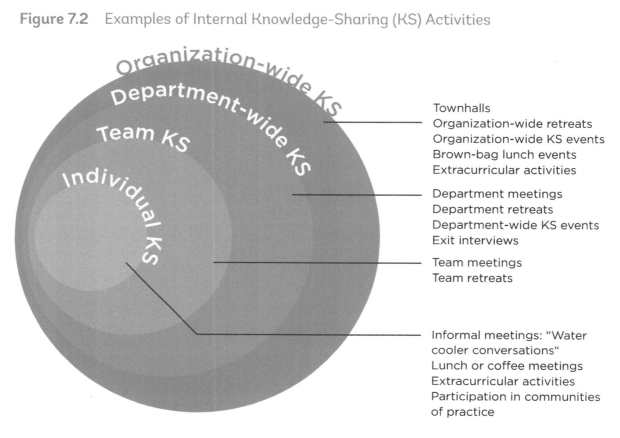

Townhalls
Organization-wide retreats
Organization-wide KS events
Brown-bag lunch events
Extracurricular activities

Department meetings
Department retreats
Department-wide KS events
Exit interviews

Team meetings
Team retreats

Informal meetings: "Water cooler conversations"
Lunch or coffee meetings
Extracurricular activities
Participation in communities of practice

Knowledge sharing can be a powerful mechanism to invigorate cross-team collaboration and spark innovation. It does not take much for knowledge sharing to happen, but organizations must nurture it to obtain its maximum value. Earlier in this guide we discussed creating an enabling environment for knowledge sharing; in what follows, we will look at a range of "quick wins" and simple techniques to encourage it (figure 7.2). After all, knowledge sharing happens best when it is fun and productive rather than a burden.

7.3.1   Formal meetings and events

Team and department meetings

Successful teams get together on a regular basis to update each other on recent events and lessons learned and go over upcoming activities. It is important to strike a balance between the team members' need for information and the time invested in such meetings. Regular team or department meetings should not become too long and can be at times just a short check-in. It is good practice to prepare a brief agenda for the meeting and send out any supporting materials in advance to ensure that all salient points are covered in the given time frame. Think through how often the group should get together, and consider the potentially longer time required for individual meetings when they are less frequent.

Townhalls

Townhalls, encompassing large departments or the entire organization, usually have two objectives: (1) allow senior management to update the staff on strategic decisions or mission-critical news and (2) receive feedback from staff members regarding the announcements; indeed, townhalls are usually most successful when they are interactive and allow for feedback and discussion. The meeting should not be longer than two hours. After the meeting, make sure that supporting documents, presentations, decision notes, and follow-up actions are shared with the participants. Strategy decisions, action steps, and roles should be clear to all. If certain strategic decisions have not yet been made, openly communicate so.

Knowledge-sharing events

Successful organizations invite a department or speaker to share recent experiences and findings that may be relevant for other staff members. These talks can cover, for example, a recent workshop or a formally produced knowledge asset and usually include time for questions and answers. The events can happen ad hoc as well as at regular intervals such as periodic lunch meetings. Make sure the events are announced well in advance through e-mails, posters, and newsletters. Keep the typical meeting short and concise—one to two hours tends to be enough for most salient questions to be covered. Think about recording sessions or using the event to trigger a more detailed capturing process.

Team retreats

Retreats can be great a way to gather staff members and engage in knowledge sharing over one or more days when important strategic decisions need to be made or critical work programs planned. A sound agenda built around clearly defined objectives is critical for a successful retreat. Some teams create a small group to plan both logistics and content. This can build ownership of the agenda and ensure that all issues important to the team are covered. The team manager may facilitate the retreat, but giving the job to a team member or an external facilitator can help in dealing with difficult questions. Make sure learnings and outcomes from the retreat are well documented and follow-up actions are clearly spelled out.

Exit interviews and knowledge-sharing events

Every organization or team will eventually lose some members of long standing as they change career paths or retire. Documenting the knowledge of these individuals through an exit interview can be critical for organizations striving to build institutional memory. In addition or alternatively, some organizations choose to organize opportunities for exiting staff members to share their knowledge with peers in a dedicated meeting or knowledge-sharing event. The exiting staff member can prepare a presentation with the learnings that he or she has built over time or just be available for questions; have someone document the key takeaways.

Knowledge Sharing in Action

Capturing and Sharing Experiences of Retiring Staff Members

Uganda's Ministry of Agriculture, Animal Industries and Fisheries

Recognizing the valuable know-how accumulated by staff members with many years of service, Uganda's Ministry of Agriculture, Animal Industries and Fisheries (MAAIF) has begun to systematically document their experiences when they declare their intention to retire. Exit interviews are captured on video and also summarized in brief lesson notes. Both formats are stored on the organization's online library of knowledge assets for quick access by anyone interested in tested solution paths developed and implemented by MAAIF veterans—including those who have retired.

7.3.2   Venues for informal knowledge sharing

Knowledge sharing often happens informally. The "water cooler conversation" is not planned but can be hugely helpful in providing a way for colleagues to quickly update one another or get advice on a current challenge to be addressed.[1] Although informal knowledge sharing is not planned, organizations have long known that it can be nurtured through thoughtful space planning.

Such planning is especially common in leading technology and research organizations. Some use open-space office layouts or furnish special meeting zones with tables, sofas, flip charts, and white boards or web-enabled smart boards. Others count spaces designed for relaxation and light recreation as conducive to knowledge sharing. A ping-pong table may not be high on the procurement list of a public sector organization, but finding ways to foster impromptu interactions between people will pay dividends.

7.3.3   Extracurricular activities

Some organizations, including India's National AIDS Control Organization (NACO) and China's Asia-Pacific Finance Development Institute, have developed centers where employees can organize extracurricular activities and socialize outside of office hours. NACO, for example, provides clubs where conversations among staff members are fostered around a good cup of Indian tea. These facilities help staff members get to know each other better as well as pursue collaborations and innovations that may not be possible in more constrained work settings.

---

[1]   The so-called water cooler conversation, initially a phenomenon in the United States, describes the spontaneous chat among employees when they run into each other in some common area of the office, such as the water fountain or kitchen. And not surprisingly, interesting connections and ideas can emerge out of such short converations and in turn facilitate deeper collaborations.

Developing Extracurricular Activities to Foster Staff Interactions

China's Asia-Pacific Finance and Development Institute

The Asia-Pacific Finance and Development Institute (AFDI), operated by China's Ministry of Finance, provides a wide range of learning offerings in China, the wider Asia-Pacific region, and beyond. To foster informal staff interactions, AFDI's management encourages employees to organize clubs and extracurricular offerings such as yoga, tennis, arts and crafts, and dancing. In such settings, conversations naturally also include work-related matters. AFDI has found that the connections made at the clubs enrich knowledge sharing between staff members and thereby help advance the organization's mission.

7.4 Practices for Domestic Knowledge Sharing

National governments seek to decrease the disparities between high- and low-performing regions in their countries. Nongovernmental organizations often find it productive to collaborate with others even if it is not part of their mandate. Domestic knowledge sharing across these public and private institutions provides a powerful way to scale up locally successful solutions and reforms and strengthen programs. The key mechanisms for such knowledge sharing are adaptation and replication. The following sections present four major phases in the process of creating a nationwide adaptation and replication program among domestic stakeholders (figure 7.3).

1. Create a facility to identify and broker needs and solutions.
2. Assess audience, needs, and objectives for each knowledge-sharing activity.
3. Implement knowledge sharing.
4. Adapt the knowledge and replicate it (or scale up) to achieve results.

Figure 7.3   Four Phases of Domestic Knowledge Sharing

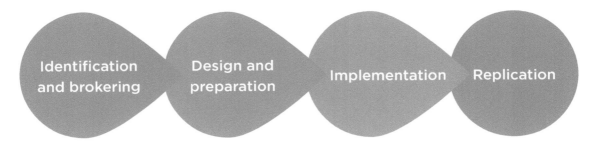

Identification and brokering

Design and preparation

Implementation

Replication

Knowledge Sharing in Action

Transferring Authority to Localities through a Knowledge-Sharing Solution

The Kenya School of Government and Knowledge Sharing on Devolution

After the 2013 elections in Kenya, the national government embarked on a far-reaching reform embedded in the 2010 constitution: devolve significant central government functions to the nation's 47 counties. The devolution agenda aims to reduce deep disparities across regions and increase social accountability. The process required new institutions at the county level as well as new responsibilities for existing local agencies. The risk inherent in the program was that the quality of local public services and governance would deteriorate under the burden of change instead of improve.

To manage the devolution process and build local agency capacity, the government asked the Kenya School of Government (KSG) to become one of several key partners for knowledge sharing and learning on devolution. KSG had a strong record of developing structured learning for the public sector in Kenya as well as in neighboring countries. Its additional role in the counties covered the creation and oversight of a peer learning platform on devolution, capturing local devolution experiences to be included in trainings, and leadership training to facilitate multistakeholder processes across the country.

The idea of systematically capturing and sharing local devolution experiences marks a tectonic shift in government thinking about the transfer of knowledge. In the traditional top-down process, national departments and schools develop and deliver local training based on a national perspective. In contrast, knowledge sharing naturally establishes a participatory approach in which local knowledge appears front and center in learning offerings. Local needs for knowledge are now increasingly being met with local experiences.

KSG is developing its capacity to act as knowledge capturer, broker, and facilitator in the devolution process. It is building a common vision and enhancing skills for its staff across all five of its campuses. If done right, the knowledge-sharing strategy for devolution promises to help reduce inequalities across counties and increase the quality of local public services in Kenya.

Early evidence is promising. Some counties that had generally been perceived as low capacity and low performing have surfaced as exemplary high performers in some areas. Their example is empowering. As counties lose the stigma of being eternal recipients of know-how and resources, knowledge increasingly flows between them.

7.4.1   Creating a facility to identify and broker needs and solutions

Before an organization begins facilitating any knowledge-sharing activities it must get a good sense of the supply and demand for knowledge. Networks and partnerships between central and local levels can help reveal "who needs to know what" and "who knows what." That information would ideally be collected by a central organization to broker just-in-time knowledge-sharing activities. The central organization might create an online platform in which seekers and providers can identify and choose each other directly (figure 7.4).

A version of such a platform was developed by Indonesia's disaster management authority (BNPB) as a mobile-phone-based "Disaster Management Solutions Finder" (see chapter 2). It allows local disaster management officials to quickly access solutions developed by peers in other parts of the country that may be relevant to their own circumstances.

Other organizations may use communities of practice, online forums, or wikis to support the brokering of knowledge. More traditional formats can also include face-to-face instruments such as conferences and multistakeholder meetings, although these are usually confined to a specific time and place and thus not continuously accessible and expandable.

The following questions may be helpful in determining what type of platform your organization would wish to develop.

» What would be the value of the knowledge-sharing platform for stakeholders in your given field of practice?

A knowledge platform on policy implementation experiences across the country might improve policy implementation by local governments, as was the case for Nigeria's Ministry of Agriculture and Rural Development, which built a mobile web application to distribute news and policy information to stakeholders (see chapter 2).

Figure 7.4   The Knowledge-Brokering Platform

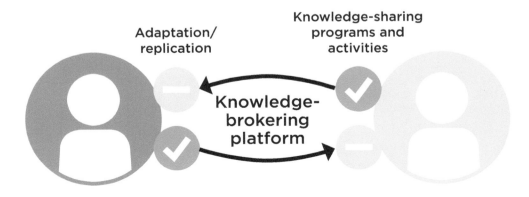

Adaptation/ replication

Knowledge-sharing programs and activities

Knowledge-brokering platform

» Who are the stakeholders that would need to access the platform?

It is essential to get a clear picture of the target audience for a knowledge-sharing platform. The needs and means of local government officials may differ from, say, those of extension workers in remote rural areas of the country.

» What knowledge should be presented, in what level of detail, and how?

Creating knowledge assets (chapter 5) offers one approach to capturing present and past experiences and presenting them in accessible and digestible formats. A brokering platform could also just provide initial pointers for supply and demand, for example through a map that provides basic data on who knows what and who needs to know it.

» How will stakeholders access the platform and what access restrictions may exist?

Will it be accessible through computers, smart phones, and tablets, or none of the above? Stakeholders in remote areas may face significant constraints in accessing online platforms.

7.4.2   Assessing audience, needs, and objectives

Once a match between a requester and provider of knowledge has been made, joint planning for the actual knowledge sharing becomes vital for its success. A preparatory meeting should identify concrete challenges on the requesting side and how those issues can most usefully be addressed by the providing side. The meeting can be facilitated by a neutral brokering agency, but some stakeholders may instead choose to work together directly.

Unfortunately many stakeholders embark on a study visit with little or no preparation on either side. Such activities commonly fail to yield the desired outcomes: the knowledge requester does not form specific questions about the challenges they face, and hence the knowledge provider does not prepare a well-targeted program. The result is often hours or days of generic presentations, a painful experience for both sides.

In a planning meeting the parties can develop a mutual understanding of the objectives of particular audience groups, their concrete needs, and the means of presentation. As stakeholders may be dispersed across the country, it may be more cost-effective to initially bring them together in a conference call or videoconference.

Some organizations—including Korea's national statistical agency (KOSTAT) and the Lagos, Nigeria, transit agency (LAMATA)—send out a questionnaire before even agreeing to a planning meeting (see appendix D.2 for a generic knowledge-sharing preparation questionnaire).

The design of the knowledge-sharing program should be guided by the objectives for the exchange, the nature of the specific audiences, and constraints such as budget, availability of participants, overall political enabling environment, and access to technology (see box 7.1).

Knowledge-sharing programs can draw on a great variety of instruments and activities, including study tours, knowledge fairs, meetings for communities of practice, multistakeholder dialogues, and conferences. An instrument may consist of several activities. For example, the instrument of a study tour may consist of activities such as introductory presentations, field visits, Q&A sessions, action

Box 7.1   Typical Constraints on Knowledge Sharing

» **Budget.** Knowledge exchange costs vary dramatically. A series of virtual dialogues can be quite inexpensive, whereas an elaborate study tour involving participants from across the country can be very costly (figure B7.1.1).

» **Time.** People tend to underestimate the time it takes to plan and complete a knowledge exchange and the number of variables involved, including the level of complexity and the nature of the outcomes sought.

» **Location and operating environment.** Common contextual constraints include political transition, civil unrest, cultural and social norms, and language. It helps to be aware of all these when dealing with recipients and providers.

» **Technology and planning resources.** Technology and guidance tools can be enormously useful, but not everyone has the same level of access, familiarity, or ability to use them.

» **People.** People include everyone involved in the exchange. Common constraints revolve around availability, willingness to participate, number of participants, preparedness, staffing, familiarity with the subject matter or a technology, ability to take action, absorptive capacity, role in the organization, and travel.

Figure B7.1.1   Physical and Personal Constraints on Knowledge Sharing (KS)

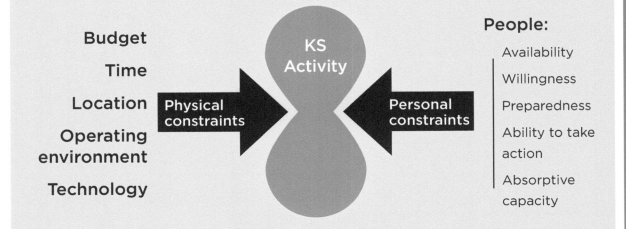

planning sessions, and informal get-togethers, all of which will require careful planning to ensure that learning happens as a result. A wide variety of options for knowledge-sharing instruments and activities can be found in the accompanying guide *The Art of Knowledge Exchange* (World Bank 2015, 83–164).

In budgeting face-to-face programs, travel and accommodation are usually the costliest elements. Significantly more cost-effective are virtual exchanges via telephone, video, and web.

Design the knowledge exchange with representatives from all parties involved. If all stakeholders are involved in planning and can influence the program design, chances are higher that the program will meet their expectations. This in turn will increase the chance of favorable feedback and concrete outcomes.

7.4.3   Implementing the knowledge-sharing program

Once the objectives are clear, the right audiences have been identified, and the design of the program agreed upon, the knowledge-sharing program moves into its implementation stage. Organizers should keep a close eye on the following areas:

» **Invitations.** Send them out well in advance.

» **Advance distribution of background documents.** Having key issues, agendas, and technical documents in the hands of participants before the program will help maximize the amount of time spent on the intended knowledge exchange.

» **Travel and transportation (if any).** Factor in travel times and distances to ensure that all participants are present for the entire duration of the exchange program.

» **Accommodation and meals (if any).** Book accommodations well in advance and as close to the knowledge-sharing venue as possible (or co-locate them). Beware of last-minute cancellation policies to keep costs low, and make sure special meal requests can be accommodated.

» **Allowances and per diems (if any).** Practices in some developing countries may call for organizers to pay allowances for out-of-town travel. In some cases, development partners may also provide allowances or vouchers for meals and transport.

» **Venue.** Check the venue carefully for handicapped accessibility, room size, seating arrangements, and all technology capabilities.

» **Interpreters and sign language.** Simultaneous or consecutive interpretation or signing for the deaf may be needed. This can involve significant costs because it involves at least two interpreters (and signers if applicable) and special audio equipment.

» **Administrative support.** Provide adequate coverage for participant registration and ad hoc and emergency needs.

» **Rapporteurs.** Assign rapporteurs for note taking and summarizing the major discussions and findings.

Remain flexible throughout the knowledge-sharing program. Consider the agenda to be a guide, not a straightjacket. As your program unfolds, the emergence of new priorities and unforeseen circumstances may require you to adjust. As long as the changes are agreed upon by the participants and well communicated, there is little risk to adapting. In fact, in most cases participants will appreciate the effort to adjust the program to their needs.

7.4.4   Adapting and replicating to achieve results

Knowledge sharing is not an end but a means to adapt and replicate successful solution paths. It is thus important to see a knowledge-sharing program not as a single event but rather as a stepping stone to achieve results. Yet this most critical step—*following up for concrete action*—is often the weakest link in the knowledge-sharing cycle.

Therefore, a knowledge-sharing program should have a results-oriented design, including concrete goals and objectives and action-planning modules that define specific next steps for the participants. The more detail in terms of milestones, delivery dates, and accountabilities, the more likely is follow-up.

Here are five key actions for effective follow-up (figure 7.5):

1. **Coordinate: establish an implementation group** responsible for implementation of the action plan. This team can course-correct if some plans prove to be unrealistic or require adaptation. Its mandate should include monitoring and evaluation.

2. **Create buy-in: convey action plans to senior managers** who have not already been involved in the knowledge-sharing activity. It is senior management that must create the favorable enabling environment for the proposed changes.

3. **Communicate: inform all stakeholders** who will be affected by implementation of the solutions. Buy-in of those not already aware of the program will be critical to successful implementation.

4. **Build capacity: conduct a capacity assessment** as needed to ensure that implementation partners have the needed skills and competencies to deliver on the identified action items.

Figure 7.5 Five Key Actions for Effective Follow-up to Knowledge Sharing

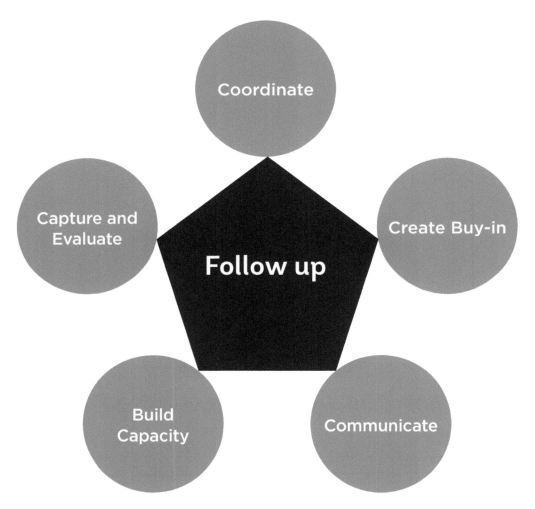

Additional support from the knowledge supply side or other actors may be required to bring all participants up to speed, although additional capacities may also be required on the supply side. Many knowledge-sharing organizations see their role as limited to the sharing phase, but some degree of support from the supply side in the action phase, for example through advisory services or technical assistance, may be critical for success.

5. **Capture and evaluate:** Capture implementation challenges and solutions. Evaluate the results for lessons that can be applied for further scale-up domestically or internationally.

7.5   Practices for International Knowledge Sharing

Organizations that excel at internal and domestic knowledge sharing will likely have no difficulties in conducting international knowledge-sharing programs—the four steps outlined above for domestic programs all apply for international exchanges. However, the first of the four, "creating a facility to identify and broker needs and solutions" merits additional attention in the international context. That is, who identifies relevant solutions, how can country institutions more effectively position themselves as knowledge hubs for their peers around the world, and what is the role of international organizations in brokering knowledge-sharing partnerships?

Leave time for extracurricular activities. Visiting participants in an international knowledge-sharing event may have never been to the host country and will likely want to use the opportunity to get to know it a bit more. Unless you leave adequate space in the agenda for them to do some sightseeing or shopping, you may unnecessarily reduce participation even in key sessions.

7.5.1   International platforms for sectoral knowledge

A variety of platforms specialize in sharing sector-specific knowledge and solutions:

» Practitioner networks gather in online communities of practice (CoP) to exchange the latest findings from research and practical experiences.

» A host of international conferences provide opportunities to network, discuss, and share.

» Massive open online courses (MOOCs) and open learning platforms increasingly provide advanced opportunities for learning and sharing at scale.

» Social media have become a powerful conduit for knowledge sharing.

» Communities of practice exist to facilitate knowledge sharing and promote practical solutions. These include the World Bank's global CoP on Learning from Megadisasters[2] and the Africa Platform for Development Effectiveness (APDev).[3]

Nonetheless, sectoral solutions remain scattered, and finding them often depends on the initiatives of individuals who choose to engage in knowledge platforms.

---

[2]   https://collaboration.worldbank.org/groups/learning-from-megadisasters.

[3]   Coordinated by the New Partnership for Africa's Development (NEPAD, a technical body of the African Union), http://www.africa-platform.org.

7.5.2   International partnerships

Many organizations engage in a variety of international partnerships that help share experiences across national boundaries. Bilateral partnerships, participation in sector networks, and partnerships with multilateral organizations can open up important learning opportunities for country institutions. Indeed, along with financing and technical assistance, knowledge sharing has become the third leg of development cooperation efforts in the international arena. United Nations organizations[4] and multilateral development banks conduct knowledge brokering across national boundaries and are well-placed to match the supply and demand for development solutions.

The World Bank Group's global practices and country teams support knowledge sharing as an integral part of projects. Through its Global Delivery Initiative (see chapter 5, box 5.1), the World Bank Group and partners such as the German Agency for International Cooperation (GIZ), the Korea Development Institute, and the Inter-American Development Bank support countries in more systematic leveraging of knowledge to improve the outcomes of development interventions. The World Bank Group's Organizational Knowledge Sharing (OKS) Program supports institutional capacity development for knowledge capturing and sharing, including the processes and strategies outlined in this handbook.[5] Multidonor trust funds, such as the South-South Facility,[6] provide just-in-time financing for design and implementation of knowledge-exchange programs.

In the advanced economies, GIZ and the United Kingdom's Department for International Development provide knowledge-sharing support. Moreover, national institutions in middle-income countries are increasingly tasked with expanding their engagement in international cooperation for development. Among them are APC-Colombia, Indonesia's Ministry of Development Planning, the Korea Development Institute, and Mexico's development cooperation agency AMEXCID. These organizations also facilitate targeted knowledge sharing with the private sector.

---

[4]   Including the UN Development Programme, UNICEF, the Food and Agriculture Organization, the UN Office for South-South Cooperation, and the International Labour Organization.

[5]   The OKS website is at http://knowledgesharingfordev.org. The World Bank guide *The Art of Knowledge Exchange* (World Bank 2015) provides a step-by-step introduction to planning and designing knowledge exchanges, especially in the context of South-South partnerships.

[6]   http://wbi.worldbank.org/sske/page/about-south-south-facility.

Knowledge Sharing in Action

Documenting and Sharing Proven Development Solutions for International Adaptation and Replication

The Korea Knowledge-Sharing Program

The Korea Knowledge-Sharing Program (KSP) was launched in 2004 by the Korea Development Institute (KDI), with support from the Ministry of Strategy and Finance, but its roots are in the International Development Exchange Program, launched at the KDI by the government in 1982. Thus, when a country today seeks development guidance from the KSP, it receives the benefit of the KDI's experience gained from decades' worth of knowledge exchange and funding work.

The KSP maintains an extensive library of more than 100 detailed case studies documenting experiences in policy reform and development. A database-driven web platform (www.kdevelopedia.org) provides access to a wide array of additional resources showcasing Korea's development experiences. Besides its systematic work in creating and publishing knowledge assets and engaging in bilateral consulting, the KSP also joins with multilateral organizations and one or more developing countries in triangular cooperation projects.

7.6 Technology-Facilitated Knowledge Sharing

Organizations use a variety of information technology (IT) platforms, such as intranets, extranets, wikis, and e-discussion systems, to provide guidance and improve know-how. However, these platforms were often built with a top-down model of information transfer; to take maximum advantage of knowledge assets, they need to exploit the more complex networks involved with knowledge sharing. A starting point for evaluating the knowledge-sharing capabilities of your own organization's IT systems is to simply ask staff members whether they are making use of the various offerings, what they think is missing, and how they could be improved.

Stable access to the Internet opens up a world of opportunities for knowledge sharing. We detail here six categories of social media that can effectively complement your existing tools. Many of the tools in each category are free of charge and are also available on smart phones and tablets. They can help you to connect, inspire, update, photograph, video, and measure; see also *The Art of Knowledge Exchange* (World Bank 2015, 39).

> » **Connect** on social networks
>
> Social network tools are a great way to keep in continuous touch with your audience. You can share activities and events by posting texts, images, videos, and links. Networks such as LinkedIn, Facebook, and Google Plus let your audience rate, appreciate ("like"), and further disseminate your contributions.

» **Inspire** through communities of practice

Online CoP tools such as Jive, Ning, and WordPress are out-of-the-box platforms you can set up to create your own community on the web. They allow you to invite members who can establish profiles and view or contribute to the content (text, images, photos, audio files etc.) on a given subject matter of interest. Many include live chat, e-discussion and polling functions that further increase interaction with your audience.

» **Update** with microblogging tools

Microblogging tools such as Twitter and Blogger allow you to share brief announcements and ideas derived from operational experiences. Ideally connected to your other social media tools, they can be a powerful way to increase real-time exposure to your knowledge and activities.

» **Photograph** with picture-sharing tools

Often an image speaks more than a thousand words, and tools such as Instagram, Picasa, and Flickr let you share photos and images from your operational activities in real time. Once uploaded, they can also be shared on other social networks.

» **Video** through video-sharing sites

As covered in chapter 5, video recording can be an influential way to convey messages and share knowledge. Platforms such as YouTube, Vimeo, and Vine let you upload videos of interviews, testimonials, and other stories to be easily viewed externally. Once uploaded, they can also be shared on other social networks.

» **Measure** with social media analytics

Tools such as Hootsuite, Sysomos, and Spredfast allow you to track, measure, and analyze data from your social media efforts in real time.

7.7   Conclusion

Although, as we have noted, knowledge sharing is more of an art than a science, its success depends on important technical considerations. Whatever knowledge sharing you plan, start with listening to develop a sound understanding of the issues to be tackled and the objectives you are trying to reach. Only then can you develop an effective, participatory process to design and implement knowledge-sharing activities. If your constituents have been involved from the outset, they will own the process and are more likely to stand by its outcomes.

7.8   Checklist

Knowledge Sharing	Yes
Do we have the right mindset for sharing: Are we listening before sharing?	
Do we systematically facilitate targeted knowledge-sharing activities at all levels of our organization?	
Do we provide venues and opportunities for informal knowledge sharing?	
Are we making systematic use of social media to complement our knowledge-sharing efforts?	
Do we have a platform that facilitates local or domestic brokering of knowledge?	
Are we using a comprehensive set of knowledge-sharing instruments and activities to design targeted and results-oriented knowledge-sharing programs?	
Do we have a process to manage the implementation of knowledge-sharing programs?	
Do we have a process to follow up knowledge sharing to ensure that solutions are adapted, scaled up, and replicated?	
Are we making systematic use of international partnerships, networks, and platforms to globally access and promote solutions?	

8. MONITORING AND EVALUATION

Learning is a mostly invisible process. As Schwandt and Marquardt (1999, 58) have said, we "see results of the learning process, as opposed to the process itself." The same holds true for organizations. It is hard to tell when an organization actually learns. We may be able to perceive increased knowledge sharing throughout the organization or between teams, but whether and what individuals or teams have learned will show up only in action. Moreover, without specific effort, it is often difficult to conclusively attribute new actions to earlier knowledge sharing and learning. In short, if you have a knowledge-sharing program, how do you know whether it's working?

This is where monitoring and evaluation come in. They are the processes that tell you whether you are achieving the intended results of your knowledge-sharing initiatives and, if not, what corrective actions are needed.

Monitoring and evaluation both assess achievements, but their emphases differ:

» **Monitoring** is generally an ongoing process of information collection primarily for program management. It tends to focus on *activities*.

» **Evaluation** takes a wider and longer-term view of the entire program and involves less frequent programmatic reviews. It tends to concern itself with *outcomes*.

Covering all aspects of monitoring and evaluation is beyond the scope of this guide, but a number of critical steps are important to keep in mind when applying the discipline to knowledge-sharing programs. Some of the measures used in monitoring will be quantitative—"hard" indicators such as how often users are accessing, contributing to, or using the knowledge assets and sharing processes you have set up. To complete the monitoring picture, however, you will want to get a sense of *why* people are using the knowledge assets or *what value* they have derived from them (box 8.1). These subjective judgments represent the qualitative, "soft" measures produced by asking people about their attitudes toward the activity—for example, did it make a difference?

Outcomes—the main preoccupation of evaluation—likewise include a mix of quantitative and qualitative measures to indicate how well a project or a process achieves its stated objectives. If we understand knowledge sharing as a tool that is *integrated into* a project or process with the goal of improving it, then the success of the project or process serves as a proxy for the success of the knowledge-sharing practices it employed. The project outcomes could cover quantifiable measures

Box 8.1   Indicators for Measuring Knowledge Sharing

Developing a set of indicators, also referred to as metrics or measures, deserves close attention. Some indicators can be qualitative ("improved collaboration"), others quantitative ("reduction of time to deliver service x"). Here are some indicators—stated as targets—that are commonly used in measuring the effectiveness of knowledge sharing. Most organizations will set such targets as benchmarks to be attained in a given period of time.

Intermediate-outcome indicators

- » Improved collaboration among staff or between departments
- » Established dedicated budget for knowledge and learning
- » Established or adapted knowledge and learning governance
- » Instituted incentive mechanisms for open peer learning
- » Created or improved domestic and international partnerships
- » Improved capabilities to conduct result-oriented and relevant knowledge sharing

Result indicators

- » Scaled up solutions at the organizational level
- » Replicated solutions domestically or internationally
- » Improved service delivery
- » Registered or implemented more innovations
- » Gained efficiencies in core operations
- » Achieved greater recognition of client's knowledge-sharing capacity

such as cost reductions and qualitative results such as stakeholder-reported improvements in delivery of services. Whatever is being used to define overall project success should in turn be put to work in helping to measure success for the knowledge activity as well.

Just as knowledge sharing should be an integral part of your organization's projects and processes, monitoring and evaluation should be an integral part of the knowledge-sharing endeavor, undertaken with thoughtful, purposeful, and systematic effort right from the outset of your planning for knowledge sharing. Make each step of monitoring and evaluation clear and meaningful to your constituents. Doing so will facilitate their cooperation, which in turn will be vital to the continuing success of your knowledge-sharing program. By approaching monitoring and evaluation systematically, your organization will create a continually improving knowledge management system.

This chapter will discuss the following broad considerations regarding monitoring and evaluation: how to provide the enabling environment, planning and implementation, and characteristics of some commonly employed monitoring tools and evaluation tools.

Define your measures with your various audiences in mind. Managers who allocate resources will want to know about returns on investment. Participants will want to know whether their involvement has been worthwhile. Potential future participants will want an accessible description of the initiative's value. Success means different things to different people, so bear that in mind as you choose your measurements.

8.1   Getting Started

As for any program, the monitoring and evaluation (M&E) phase of your knowledge-sharing activities must be carefully structured and planned if it is to produce useful results. M&E requires a focus. You may want to measure improvements in operational effectiveness or the gains in the enlargement of institutional memory. Or you may seek to find out whether specific solutions have been successfully scaled up.

8.1.1   Establishing the enabling environment

With an initial sense of the goals for your M&E effort, you can turn to the specific elements of the enabling environment required to make it happen. Here are some to consider:

Overall responsibility

Who is in charge of the monitoring and evaluation tasks? Are there additional decision makers?

The governance of M&E should be defined from the outset. Some possibilities:

- » A centralized model in which M&E is handed to one manager or expert
- » An evaluation committee, possibly consisting of representatives from different departments in your organization
- » An advisory group, a more loosely organized group of experts or quality champions who can provide guidance without any formal decision-making authority

For committees, some organizations opt for regular meetings in which the knowledge and learning activities are discussed and progress monitored. In chapter 5, we discussed the validation team which can convene regularly to evaluate the quality of knowledge assets.

Implementation

Who will be responsible for implementation and do you have the in-house capabilities to follow through? M&E can require a significant investment of time. Often many stakeholder groups have to get involved, including external partners and beneficiaries of services, which means that data collection may require travel.

Partner with universities. Working with a local university can be a win-win collaboration. You will likely be able to reduce costs, and academic partners can provide technical expertise. For the university, it can be advantageous to have access to a "real life" program for research purposes. Make sure you reach full agreement on the purpose and scope of the evaluation to avoid any misunderstanding down the line.

Think through who is best suited to undertake the M&E tasks. Internal staff, outsourcing, or some combination of the two may suit your circumstances best. In some cases, peers can perform reviews. Outsourcing can come at a significant cost but may be less biased toward positive interpretations.[1] (See also chapter 5 on options for validation of knowledge assets because these also apply to other evaluation tasks.)

Funding

Monitoring and evaluation should be one of the items on your list when budgeting for knowledge sharing (see also chapter 3). But what is the right budget? Evaluations can be expensive; some of the more intricate impact evaluations of development projects can, in U.S. currency terms, cost hundreds of thousands of dollars. An initial budget may have to be larger than that for an ongoing M&E process.

The variables determining a satisfactory monitoring and evaluation process are time and expertise. The budget will determine the level of detail reached by the assessment—for example, how many questions to ask of how many people. Organizations typically assign to a program's M&E budget anywhere between 5 and 20 percent of the program's cost.

Your budget will likely need to include some or all of the following:

> » Personnel costs (both in-house and outsourced)

> » Travel

---

[1] Some experts argue, however, that the benefits of an independent evaluation are at times exaggerated. See the blog post by Howard White, "Is Independence Always a Good Thing?" May 1, 2014, http://blogs.3ieimpact.org/is-independence-always-a-good-thing.

» Event costs

» Materials and supplies

» Communications

» Indirect costs or overhead

Refine your budget over time. Budgeting for monitoring and evaluation is an iterative process, and you will likely have to adapt your budget as new data become available. Start your budgeting with a detailed list of all expected costs based on your best estimate, and refine it further as you move toward more detailed planning and implementation.

Quality standards

Monitoring and evaluation can provide the necessary data for management to make informed decisions about internal operations if the information is of sufficiently high quality. The UN Development Programme's independent evaluation office has defined a set of norms for its evaluation policy. These norms, which also apply to evaluations of knowledge-sharing programs, consist of the following eight characteristics (with descriptions drawn from their website):[2]

» **Independence.** The evaluation function should be structurally independent from the operational management and decision-making functions in the organization so that it is free from undue influence, more objective, and has full authority to submit reports directly to appropriate levels of decision making. Management must not impose restrictions on the scope, content, comments, and recommendations of evaluation reports.

» **Intentionality.** The rationale for an evaluation and the decisions to be based on it should be clear from the outset. The scope, design, and plan of the evaluation should generate relevant, timely products that meet the needs of intended users.

» **Transparency.** Meaningful consultation with stakeholders is essential for the credibility and utility of the evaluation. Full information on evaluation design and methodology should be shared throughout the process to build confidence in the findings and understanding of their limitations in decision making.

» **Ethics.** Evaluations should not reflect personal or sectoral interests. Evaluators must have professional integrity and respect the rights of institutions and individuals to provide information in confidence and to verify statements attributed to them.

---

[2] http://web.undp.org/evaluation/policy.shtml.

» **Impartiality.** Criteria to foster impartiality are independence from management, objective design, valid measurement and analysis, and the rigorous use of appropriate benchmarks agreed upon beforehand by all stakeholders.

» **Quality.** The key questions and areas of investigation should be clear, coherent, and realistic and the information generated accurate and reliable.

» **Timeliness.** Evaluations should be designed and implemented in a timely fashion to be relevant and useful.

» **Utility.** The scope, design, and plan of the evaluation should generate relevant, timely products that meet the needs of intended users.

8.2 From Planning to Implementing

Evaluations typically fit into one of three types—positive deviance, participatory evaluation, or horizontal evaluation (box 8.2). The treatment here addresses mainly horizontal evaluations, but many of the concepts would also apply to the other two. Here is a three-step process that will base the execution of your M&E process on sound planning (figure 8.1): (1) carefully define the program you are studying, (2) choose the most appropriate method of data collection, and (3) choose an analytical approach to synthesize the measured outcomes.

Figure 8.1   The Three Basic Steps of the Monitoring and Evaluation Process

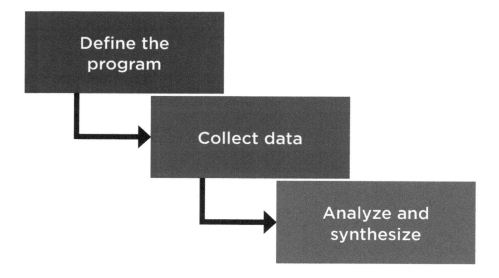

Box 8.2   What Type of Evaluation Should We Do?

Knowledge-sharing programs are typically evaluated in one of three ways: (1) positive deviance, (2) participatory evaluation, and (3) horizontal evaluation.

Positive deviance. Examining high-performance knowledge-sharing activities to understand why they are successful.

Participatory evaluation. Using evaluation processes with multiple stakeholders. By involving all key players, the output of the evaluation tasks will likely be more balanced. In addition, participatory evaluation processes also usually generate more buy-in and acceptance of the evaluation outcomes and recommendations that follow.

Horizontal evaluation. Engaging stakeholders in a structured manner, for example through interviews, focus groups, or peer learning activities.

8.2.1   Define the program you are assessing

A prerequisite of any program's assessment is a concise description of the program's objectives and activities. As M&E should be considered an inherent element of your knowledge-sharing program, the program's description should include some details on overall benefits of the M&E effort, its stakeholders, scale, and potential partners involved. It should also include the budget figures described earlier.

Try to be as specific as possible in your description of what the success of your knowledge-sharing program looks like. A simple causal chain can help to describe the theory of change underlying the program by linking activities to outcomes. A typical causal chain to describe the linkages is inputs —> activities —> outputs —> outcomes —> impact (figure 8.2). Although the format of the results chain may be a bit restrictive, it can help structure your basic thinking on causalities in your knowledge-sharing program.

Link knowledge sharing to a clear goal. Defining the purpose of knowledge-sharing programs from the outset is critical. What constitutes success? And when do we know we have achieved our goals? Develop a goal statement early on, and define some indicators that help to describe the desired change in concrete and measurable terms.

Figure 8.2 Causal Chain That Links Inputs to Impact

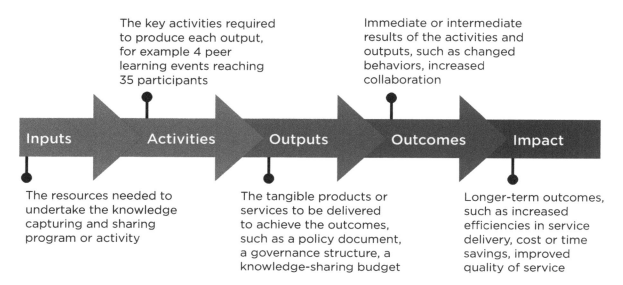

The key activities required to produce each output, for example 4 peer learning events reaching 35 participants

Immediate or intermediate results of the activities and outputs, such as changed behaviors, increased collaboration

Inputs → Activities → Outputs → Outcomes → Impact

The resources needed to undertake the knowledge capturing and sharing program or activity

The tangible products or services to be delivered to achieve the outcomes, such as a policy document, a governance structure, a knowledge-sharing budget

Longer-term outcomes, such as increased efficiencies in service delivery, cost or time savings, improved quality of service

8.2.2 Collect data

To understand what happened and what outcomes were achieved, you will need to ask the stakeholders who were directly or indirectly involved in (or affected by) the knowledge-sharing activity. If asking everybody who falls into that category is uneconomic, you will have to define a sample that will allow you to draw conclusions for the larger population.

Here are three approaches to sample selection:

» Probability sampling, for example by selecting clusters of target groupings or random sampling.

» Purposeful sampling, which focuses on a selection of target audiences based on specific criteria.

» Convenience sampling, a design driven by the accessibility of the sample group. This will often be the most economic option but may not always yield credible conclusions.

Here are four approaches to collecting data from your sample:

» **Ask individuals.** Organizations can use opinion polls, questionnaires, online surveys, interviews, diaries and many other methods to collect information from individuals. Some of these techniques are discussed later in this chapter in the sections on "Monitoring Tools" and "Evaluation Tools."

» **Ask groups.** The most widely used way to collect information from groups is through focus groups. But after-action reviews and other participatory techniques, such as group brainstorming or world cafés, can also be useful if seeking feedback from larger groups.

» **Observe.** Observing the impact of knowledge sharing on, for example, replication of a solution can be an adequate way to gather insights on its effectiveness. Field trips, photography, or video recording can support observation activities by documenting behavior of relevant target audiences.

» **Review existing records and data.** Sometimes existing documents, records, and reports of past activities and outputs can provide a good basis for evaluating their potential effect on results. Increasingly, journals, diaries, blog posts, and e-discussions are documenting activities on a nearly continuous basis.

Save costs. You may be tempted to find out everything under the sun about the effectiveness of your knowledge-sharing efforts. But focusing on the essential data can be a significant cost saver because it reduces data collection and processing time. Another way to reduce costs may be by reducing the sample size. Think through how many stakeholders are needed to provide a good enough idea of results. Lastly you may want to use online tools such as web-based surveys to collect data or organize videoconference-based focus groups and phone interviews.

8.2.3   Analyze and synthesize

Analysis is the moment when both numeric and qualitative data are summarized and correlations and patterns are identified. In the context of knowledge sharing, much of the information reviewed by the data analysis team will likely be qualitative, such as questionnaire responses and interview recordings. Sometimes it can be helpful to structure the data into a two-dimensional matrix: (1) main issues or topics and (2) cases or examples where they have been addressed. The issues or topics go into the columns and cases or examples into the rows. The intersecting cells mark the relevant findings from each experience or case per topic.

Unwarranted assumptions can be tricky to handle when it comes to evaluation tasks. A common area in which they arise is attributing causality to the knowledge-sharing activity regarding positive outcomes when other, unexamined factors may have been more decisive. In such cases it will be useful to identify such potential factors and possibly rule them out. One approach is to check whether the collected data are consistent with your expectation prior to the evaluation. You can also assess how the intended result might have been different in the absence of the knowledge-sharing activity. More elaborate impact evaluations include control groups or comparison groups that are similar to the targeted group but did not participate in the knowledge-sharing activity.

Techniques for analysis

The following of techniques can be used when analyzing evaluation data for knowledge sharing. The most common measure is the value added to an operation by a knowledge-sharing activity.

Cost-benefit analysis

The cost-benefit analysis compares the total costs incurred by a knowledge-sharing activity to the benefits it created, all usually expressed in monetary terms. What sounds simple can in reality be quite complicated because the underlying assumption—that a monetary value can be assigned to all the costs and, especially, all the benefits of knowledge sharing—may not be true. For example, measuring the net present value of collaboration across teams,[3] or the benefit derived when a new staff member is brought on board more smoothly can be inherently difficult. Many of the benefits of knowledge sharing remain somewhat intangible. One question to ask when determining the monetary value of knowledge sharing is, what would be the cost of not doing it?

Cost-effectiveness analysis

Cost-effectiveness analysis is also a common type that gauges cost, but it avoids the problem of assigning monetary value to the benefits of knowledge sharing. Instead, it adds up directly measurable costs and compares them to physical, nonmonetary outcomes such as "increase in tons per hectare of rice harvested" or "reduction in HIV/AIDS prevalence." The cost-effectiveness ratio is computed by dividing the total measureable costs of the knowledge-sharing activity by the physical units of accomplishment. The result yields quantities such as, say, $X per ton of increased rice production or $Y per 1 percentage point reduction in HIV/AIDS prevalence. Applying cost-effectiveness analysis to several similar programs, only some of which included knowledge sharing, is another way to obtain insights into effectiveness.

Carefully design cost-benefit and cost-effectiveness analyses of knowledge sharing. Start with a comprehensive list of knowledge-sharing costs that could arise, ideally based on the budget developed. Take an equally comprehensive approach to listing all potential benefits. Cooperative design is crucial for these types of analysis. Control groups may vary significantly in their sensitivity to certain benefits; and an incomplete accounting may obscure some important aspects of knowledge-sharing effectiveness.

Numeric weighting

Numeric weighting can be a very quick and simple way to assess the effectiveness of knowledge sharing. A target group rates (on a scale of 1 to 5, for example) the level of success in reaching each of several effectiveness criteria, such as "increased performance," "improved service delivery," and so on. The ratings are then summed for each criterion (which are then sometimes weighted according to their importance), and those totals are summed to create a total score for the entire

---

[3]   The net present value of knowledge sharing is the sum of the discounted benefits of all knowledge-sharing activities minus their discounted costs as of the same measurement date.

knowledge-sharing activity. The downside of this methodology is that the scores represent only the subjective assessments of the participants. However, this technique is useful to get a quick idea of stakeholder impressions of performance.

Synthesis

Once you are done with the analysis, you may be able to draw some more general conclusions regarding the effectiveness of the knowledge-sharing activity. These conclusions may support a recommendation to apply knowledge sharing to similar programs in the near future. But be sure the conditions are comparable. A successful knowledge-sharing program in one area may fail in another if, for example, similar management support is lacking.

Make monitoring and evaluation part of your communication strategy. Reporting is a key component of the evaluation process, and sharing the findings of your evaluation have to be carefully thought through. At the very beginning, define and select your audience and how they can benefit from the evaluation. Share the report widely, in staff meetings, conferences, and the organization's internal platform. Producing a short video with some compelling stories and interviews can do wonders in getting your colleagues' attention. Additional flyers, posters, short results stories, and infographics can enrich your communication mix.

8.3   Monitoring Tools

8.3.1   Post-event satisfaction survey

Collecting the opinions and impressions of knowledge users and of participants in knowledge-sharing events should be a standard component of your organization's knowledge strategies and products. Even short, simple surveys in the wake of an event will help build a database for ultimately evaluating the initiative. Surveys also communicate to your audience your commitment to improving the knowledge-sharing program.

8.3.2   Opinion polls

Opinion polls can help gauge where a target group stands on a specific issue. Opinion polls usually use a random sample of the population. They will generally involve a larger group of stakeholders and can become time consuming and quite costly. The universe of participants can consist of those who have had time to reflect on a specific action or issue before being questioned or those who have not had time to reflect in advance, but the groups are generally not mixed.

8.3.3   Diaries

Diaries and outcome journals allow for recording and monitoring data on outcomes over longer periods. They are a self-assessment tool that allows involved stakeholders to keep track of what happened, which outputs were generated, and how they have contributed, or were intended to contribute, to a result. A typical outcome journal includes a description of the challenge and a list of indicators that measure whether progress has been made, including when, where, and by whom.

If you decide to log activities, make your entries right after the event because important details may otherwise be forgotten. Also, carefully consider the format of your journal; an "anything goes" or unstructured approach will likely reduce its utility when it comes time to review and extract information.

8.3.4   After-action reviews

After-action reviews are meetings conducted by organizers—or organizers plus participants—at the conclusion of a project or activity to analyze successes and failures in an open and honest fashion. A typical after-action meeting (which may be aided by a facilitator) begins with a restatement of the scope of the activity followed by a structured series of questions that might go as follows:

1. What was supposed to happen? What actually happened?

2. Why were there differences?

3. What worked, what didn't, and why?

4. What should we do differently next time?

The facilitator may solicit quantitative data related to cost management as well as qualitative data such as perceived quality of the end product. As noted in chapter 5, these reviews represent a technique for knowledge assessment when conducted following operational activities. In that context, the review would ideally include all members of the team involved in the operation, or at least those present during its execution. The review can be conducted after any knowledge-sharing activity or even after the creation of a knowledge asset. For a knowledge-sharing activity, the review would typically encompass the organizers, and the results would be fed into the evaluation phase; the participants' reactions would be captured by other techniques such as surveys (see appendix D.3 for a report template).

8.3.5   Web-based survey tools

The many well-designed survey tools available on the Internet can ease the burden of survey design, implementation, and collection. Relative to traditional survey methods, web-based platforms (such as SurveyMonkey.com) allow you to reach a broader audience in a shorter period with a higher level of detail and orderliness. Furthermore, if the number of your responses is not especially large, many of these platforms are free of charge. For participants in areas with weak Internet access, the web-based survey can be supplemented with phone interviews or other means. This method is further discussed below under "Evaluation Tools."

8.3.6   Most-significant change

The most-significant change (MSC) tool is a form of participatory monitoring and evaluation by the stakeholders in a knowledge-sharing activity. It begins with the collection and systematic selection of success stories from field operations, which are then evaluated by panels of designated stakeholders or staff. These evaluators sit down together, read the stories aloud, and have regular and often in-depth discussions about the value of these reported changes.

The MSC process occurs throughout the knowledge-sharing program cycle and informs program management. Like other monitoring tools, it provides data on impact and outcomes that can be used to help assess the performance of the program as a whole. One advantage of the MSC process is that stories from the field can yield unanticipated insights and allow for a more dynamic evaluation process. The information generated may also be useful to the process of validating specific knowledge assets.

8.4   Evaluation Tools

8.4.1   Questionnaires

Questionnaires or surveys may be the most common way to collect data for the purpose of evaluation (see also "Web-based survey tools," above, in the section on monitoring tools). Questionnaires can be disseminated in numerous ways ranging from real-time administration in a face-to-face setting to online and mobile questionnaires. The latter choices are becoming a common and increasingly popular way to collect data, as they permit relatively quick assembly, dissemination, and administration of the survey.

Specialized survey and polling software helps reduce the cost of data entry, which is especially relevant when dealing with larger sample sizes. The data is instantaneously available and reminders can be sent with a simple click of a button. Additional advantages include the automation of "skip patterns" (presenting some questions only if the respondent has answered a previous one), a scheme that is sometimes difficult to employ in paper-based surveys. A variation of Internet-based surveys is the use of questionnaires that use smart phones and dedicated apps for data collection. These surveys can capture data on the location of the users to allow for geospatial mapping of all data points. On the downside, Internet and mobile applications limit the sample to populations that have access to the Internet or mobile data connections, and questions cannot easily be tested or clarified.

8.4.2   Balanced scorecard

In contrast to traditional accounting-oriented measures for business, the balanced scorecard adds three intangible success factors to the financial dimension: the customer or service recipient, internal processes, and learning or growth (Kaplan and Norton 1996). The advantage of this augmented business-oriented approach for evaluating knowledge sharing is that it directly links learning to operational performance, which in turn is linked with overall organizational performance. The balanced scorecard can thus provide important insights into staff motivation and capabilities, supporting systems, and processes. Many organizations, especially in the private sector, use software to integrate the balanced scorecard into their performance management processes.

8.4.3 Retrospective outcome assessment

This approach, also referred to as "outcome harvesting," retrospectively describes the context, the project, the key actors, and the behaviors involved in a knowledge-sharing initiative; how these elements changed over time; and what influences the initiative had in changing keys behaviors. Interestingly, a retrospective outcome assessment quite frequently also reveals outcomes that were not initially intended. The assessment involves three main phases:

1. Reviewing reports, papers, and conversations with initiative staff and stakeholders

2. Creating a timeline of the initiative using the compiled information to describe the contributions of the project

3. Identifying key actors in the timeline and contacting them to further assess the initiative's contribution to change

Conduct a relevant analysis that you can communicate clearly. As you prepare to analyze and present the results of your evaluation, be sure to refer back to your original goals and the primary interests of your audience. The aim of your evaluation should be to present results that answer key questions in a meaningful way, avoiding a complex mix of facts and figures.

8.5   Conclusion

Monitoring and evaluation is a critical aspect of knowledge sharing that will greatly contribute to its long-term success. It can provide the accountability for resources spent, the basis for practical improvement in knowledge sharing, and the validation of the learning being accomplished. These contributions are vital if the growth of knowledge sharing and its increasing visibility in the agendas of national and international policy makers is to be sustained.

8.6   Checklist

Monitoring and Evaluation	Yes
Are we systematically measuring the outcomes of our knowledge sharing within the organization?	
Are we systematically measuring the outcomes of our external knowledge sharing?	
Have we defined clear roles and responsibilities for our monitoring and evaluation?	
Have we budgeted for our monitoring and evaluation?	
Have we clearly defined our monitoring and evaluation program, for example by creating a causal chain that links our investments in knowledge sharing to outcomes and impact?	
Have we established a sound data collection process?	
Have we selected appropriate techniques for data analysis and synthesis?	

9. SUMMING UP: BECOMING A KNOWLEDGE-SHARING ORGANIZATION

Knowledge Sharing in Action

Getting Started: Developing a Knowledge-Sharing Initiative

Uganda's Ministry of Agriculture, Animal Industry and Fisheries

In 2014, Uganda's Ministry of Agriculture, Animal Industry and Fisheries (MAAIF) asked the World Bank to help it establish knowledge sharing as an integral part of the ministry's operations. Its goal was to systematically identify, capture, and share its solutions for improving agricultural and fisheries productivity domestically and with international peers.

The World Bank started with workshops and meetings aimed at building a common understanding of the goal and the path for getting there. One of the first such meetings assembled participants from all departments to assess the organization's knowledge-sharing strengths and gaps using indicators from the World Bank's Knowledge-sharing Capability Framework.

In a second step, a multidisciplinary team from MAAIF agreed on key milestones for mainstreaming knowledge sharing in the ministry's core operations and visually represented them as a road map. In a participatory process with the director in charge of knowledge sharing and staff from all departments, the team then developed a knowledge-sharing vision for the organization.

In a third step, the multidisciplinary team identified a set of priority actions to be tackled within 100 days:

> » Establish a task force to draft a knowledge-sharing strategy with specified elements:
>
>   o Defined roles and responsibilities
>
>   o A budget creation process

> o   Partnerships strategy
>
> o   Incentive mechanisms
>
> »   Get input from stakeholders on the draft strategy
>
> »   Submit the draft strategy for top-management approval
>
> MAAIF used a rapid-results methodology to define milestones, targets, roles, and responsibilities to ensure timely implementation. Within three months, MAAIF established the task force that in turn developed the strategy document in a workshop facilitated by the World Bank, developed the budget, and received approval by the minister.

The preceding chapters point the way to creating a knowledge-sharing culture in your organization. This chapter consolidates their essential messages into steps that encompass two stages: "building the foundation" (chapters 1–4) and "executing the program" (chapters 5–8). These steps convey a bird's-eye view of the change process needed to get the ball rolling and keep it rolling (figure 9.1). World Bank programs delivering active, onsite support are mentioned in the steps where applicable.

Some steps may best be done in parallel or in a different order, and as always, specific details will vary greatly from organization to organization—just keep these steps in mind as you design your own process.

The monitoring and evaluation step is next to last, but—like chapter 8 itself—perhaps it should be read first. It emphasizes a critical mindset and rigorous procedure that must be built in from the very beginning of the change process and continued throughout the operation of the knowledge-sharing program.

Figure 9.1   Stages of the Knowledge-Sharing (KS) Journey

Building the foundation

1. Create a KS coordination team
2. Create a vision and expectations
3. Assess your organization's KS capabilities
4. Create the strategy
5. Develop pilot programs
6. Define success measures
7. Establish a governance structure
8. Develop communications
9. Formulate a budget
10. Develop partnerships

Executing the program

1. Develop knowledge capturing and sharing skills
2. Develop a KS platform
3. Capture experiences
4. Implement the KS pilots
5. Develop learning offerings
6. Measure outcomes
7. Scale up

The knowledge-sharing journey

9.1   Building the Foundation

As outlined in chapters 1 through 4, establishing knowledge sharing in your organization requires leadership by a committed group of people. Outside facilitators can be useful in building the foundation for knowledge sharing. The World Bank works with seasoned partners in all regions to provide support services for organizations that wish to put themselves on track to become a knowledge-sharing organization.

In building the foundation, the leadership group leads a *collaborative* process involving the entire organization to

- » Create a knowledge-sharing coordination team
- » Create a vision and expectations
- » Assess your organization's knowledge-sharing capabilities
- » Create the strategy
- » Develop pilot programs
- » Define success measures
- » Establish a governance structure
- » Develop communications and build excitement
- » Formulate a budget
- » Develop partnerships

9.1.1   Create a knowledge-sharing coordination team

Step one is creating a committed group within your organization, a knowledge-sharing coordination team. This team will consist of your "change agents," so as you select them, be sure they are advocates who also have the standing—formal or informal—to influence a wider audience.

Who will you need? Usually senior management must be involved from the start, ideally spearheading the effort. Be aware, however, that the process will be unnecessarily rocky if middle-management support and involvement are missing in the early stages. You will also need technical staff and opinion leaders on board. Finally, be sure to immediately engage any knowledge management and IT experts, as they are the most likely to be champions of the change.

The members of your knowledge-sharing coordination team will be the knowledge-sharing champions, natural enthusiasts who lead by example and inspire others. As the heart of the knowledge-sharing effort, they will take it throughout the organization. Hence, they should likewise come from all parts of the institution. Depending on the size of your organization, they could well number up to 30 people, but probably not more.

9.1.2   Create a vision and expectations

The knowledge-sharing coordination team should take the lead in making knowledge sharing the default behavior of the organization, embedding it in the actions of senior management and in all operations. An essential part of doing that is creating a short but concrete vision statement embodying the goals and expectations of knowledge sharing. Developing it in a participatory way—by the knowledge-sharing coordination team in consultation with the rest of the staff—is the key to making it believable and creating ownership.

Focus the vision by stating what the organization's knowledge sharing should look like in three to five years and how it will support the organization's overall mission. The vision will be the anchor for the change process to come, quickly explaining to anyone inside or outside the organization what knowledge sharing aims to achieve. Discovering the obstacles and assets related to that vision comes next.

9.1.3   Assess your organization's knowledge-sharing capabilities

How much knowledge sharing is already going on in your organization? What necessary capabilities already exist and which ones need to be strengthened or created for knowledge sharing to become part of everyday life at work? A sound diagnostic is the way to find out, and now is the time. The World Bank has developed a one-day interactive, facilitated self-assessment workshop in which a group of about 20–30 staff members, including management, can jointly reflect on the organization's current capabilities with respect to the eight pillars outlined in this guide. The assessment will by no means be "scientific," but it will provide a critical reading on the strengths to build on and the gaps to be filled.

Several steps are essential for a session in which all participants are fully and honestly engaged: establish an environment of trust, declare and demonstrate that all opinions count, and keep the process light and fun. Quite often, this exercise has proven to be the first time that many participants have had the opportunity to deeply reflect on their organization's behavior and culture in a collaborative setting. So this session will go far in setting the tone for the way knowledge sharing is intended to work in the organization.

Some organizations may prefer online surveys for this assessment. Surveys can be highly inclusive, but they suffer from a lack of reflection and discussion. If you use a survey, offer a follow-up activity in which such reflection can happen. Similarly, a report by a consultant usually fails to get the deep buy-in needed by the various stakeholders.

Drawing up a table that summarizes the results of a self-assessment session is a great way to focus action (discussed next). Figure 9.2 is a summary of results drawn up by a public sector organization that held a self-assessment session. Participants rated capabilities for each pillar and for the series of enablers needed for a supportive environment. The three performance levels—superior, good, and attention (needed)—are averages of the participant ratings.

Now the necessary elements are in place for a detailed strategy that will take your organization from the status quo to the stated vision.

Figure 9.2 Knowledge-Sharing (KS) Capabilities: Summary Results of an Initial Self-Assessment at a Public Sector Organization

Pillar		Driver	Driver Score	Enablers (n=30)					
				Skills & Knowledge	Staff Motivation	Leadership Commitment	Human Resources	Financial & Material Resources	Linkages
Leadership & Culture	1	Systematic use of experience	Good	Good	Attention	Good	Superior	Good	Good
	2	Meaningful incentive system	Good						
Governance, Skills & Systems	3	Effective tools and systems	Good	Good	Attention	Attention	Superior	Attention	Good
	4	Clear roles and responsibilities	Attention						
Financing	5	Sufficient financial resources	Attention	Superior	Attention	Attention	Good	Attention	Good
Partnerships	6	KS partnerships to foster scale up	Good	Good	Attention	Good	Good	Attention	Good
Identification & Capturing	7	Effective process for identifying, validating	Good	Superior	Attention	Good	Superior	Attention	Good
Knowedge & Learning Offerings	8	Integrated participatory K&L offerings	Good	Superior	Good	Good	Superior	Attention	Good
Knowledge Sharing	9	Systematic KS to improve service delivery	Attention	Good	Good	Attention	Superior	Attention	Attention
Mentoring & Evaluation	10	Rigorous assessment of KS activities	Attention	Superior	Good	Attention	Superior	Attention	Attention

9.1.4 Create the strategy

You have the team, the vision, and a picture of where to focus the attention of the change process. Now you can tackle the design for the journey—the strategy. The strategy document is a road map and action plan, to be developed by the stakeholder team or, if the team is large, then by a subgroup. The World Bank has developed a workshop to aid the development of the strategy document by guiding key stakeholders through the three dimensions of knowledge sharing—internal, domestic, and international. The outcomes of the discussions form the basis for the strategy document, which is then drafted, shared, validated, and approved by senior management.

Figure 9.3   A Road Map for the Change-Management Process

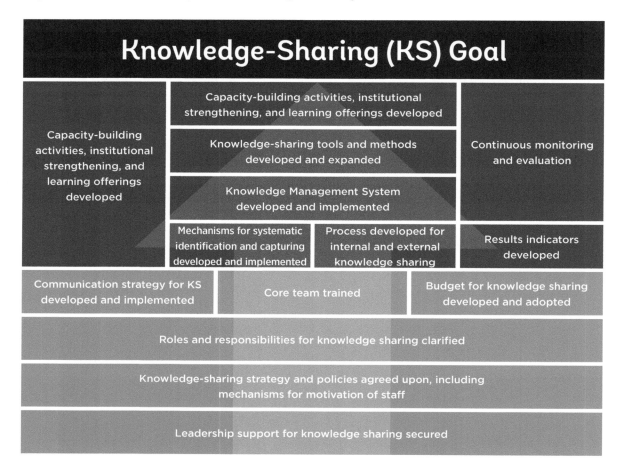

The road map will be a simple but important way to communicate the change process to all stakeholders. Create a diagram or other easily grasped outline showing the expected sequence of major milestones, with the understanding that some may have to be worked on in parallel and that the order may change along the way (figure 9.3 is such a road map, developed by another public sector organization).

The road map will be the guide for the strategy document's in-depth action plan. The action plan specifies the activities necessary to reach the milestones, and it assigns clearly defined roles and responsibilities. Depending on the duration of the overall change process, which is usually about two or three years, the plan should be highly detailed for only the initial three to six months. Subsequent activities should be in the plan but left at a more schematic level until later stages, when conditions will have evolved and the needs for the later stages are clearer.

The document should be circulated and consulted throughout the change process and revised as needed. (See appendix A.3 for an example of an actual strategy document developed by a public sector organization.)

9.1.5   Develop pilot programs

Using knowledge sharing in pilot programs can help build early buy-in for the knowledge-sharing initiative. Do it as soon as it seems feasible—the sooner you can demonstrate the value added by knowledge sharing, the better, and the lessons learned in such real-world tests are invaluable.

Depending on the strategic focus of the organization and its partnerships, the pilot can be internal, domestic, or international. Some organizations may choose to conduct one pilot at each of those levels. Choose areas that are high priority for your organization to get high visibility for the knowledge-sharing efforts and outcomes.

9.1.6   Define success measures

Monitoring and evaluation (M&E) should be a red thread that runs throughout the introduction, maintenance, and growth of your organization's knowledge-sharing program. M&E cannot function unless, at the beginning of each step discussed in this guide, (1) desired outcomes are identified along with measurable indicators of success for each outcome, against a baseline where possible (see section 9.2.6); (2) operations and intermediate results are monitored and documented; and (3) results are evaluated against goals. A sound M&E program will help keep the flame of knowledge sharing alive and demonstrate concretely how it makes the difference for an organization's performance in service delivery.

9.1.7   Establish a governance structure

Defining roles and responsibilities early in the change process creates a formal space for various actors to engage on the agenda. As noted in chapter 2, the practice of knowledge sharing will not happen without specific structures, systems, and roles to support it. The World Bank delivers workshops devoted to the design of governance for knowledge sharing, covering both existing and potential additional functions needed to deliver on the goals set for knowledge sharing.

9.1.8   Develop communications and build excitement

A big part of any change effort is communication. Many staff members will often not know about a new effort, and some who may have heard may be lukewarm about it at best. The action plan must include the communication and promotional efforts that will create excitement in the organization and demonstrate the tangible, positive impact that knowledge-sharing can have for everyone's day-to-day work. The need for strong and passionate communication cannot be overemphasized and plays a critical role in the success of the change process.

So, what can change agents do to ensure people are in the know? Senior management must openly declare support, then ask for everyone's commitment to the agenda and back that up with nonmonetary yet highly attractive incentives. Regular meetings of the core team as well as the prioritizing knowledge-sharing updates and discussion in departmental meetings will help keep the project moving.

9.1.9 Formulate a budget

The budget tells the tale—no matter what the statements and plans say, it is the budget that will reveal how seriously the organization is committed to knowledge sharing. As detailed in chapter 3, the budget will need to include labor, equipment, materials, and—where applicable—finance to show that adequate funding is available to achieve results in a given budget period.

Depending on the budget cycle of the organization, some activities that require significant funds may need to wait for the next round. However, in many cases much of the knowledge-sharing work depends on staff time, which tends to be a bit more fungible. Make sure that the budget is delivered within the required deadline and gives adequate reasoning for the various expenditures.

9.1.10 Develop partnerships

The increasingly complex environments facing public sector organizations make partnerships an important option in building up the quality and visibility of your knowledge-sharing program, both internally and externally. Domestic partnerships are important for broadening the learning horizon and for scaling up proven solutions. International partnerships can likewise increase exposure to good practice in the operational mission. Partnerships can also provide financing.

9.2 Executing the Program

Chapters 5–8 put knowledge sharing on wheels. They show how to

- » Develop knowledge capturing and sharing skills
- » Develop a knowledge-sharing platform
- » Capture experiences
- » Implement the knowledge-sharing pilots
- » Develop learning offerings
- » Measure outcomes
- » Scale up

9.2.1   Develop knowledge capturing and sharing skills

Partnerships and pilots can support the acquisition of the new skills essential to effectively identify, capture, validate, manage, and share knowledge and to continuously monitor and evaluate the program.

The World Bank has developed various guides, tools, and learning offerings to help organizations develop some of these skills and upgrade their existing programs. The World Bank team increasingly works with a network of partners across the world to take such offerings to scale.

> » A three- to four-day workshop covers the skills for systematic identification and capturing of knowledge.

> » The World Bank (2015) guide *The Art of Knowledge Exchange* introduces a five-step framework and a wide spectrum of instruments and activities to be used for knowledge sharing.

> » Another offering helps organizations design group participation and interactions into their learning offerings.

9.2.2   Develop a knowledge-sharing platform

A knowledge repository, or platform, stores knowledge. In developing the repository, think beyond a traditional website because its search and maintenance functions will likely be too limited. A database system with a proper taxonomy and an interface that is accessible from smart phones and tablets is often desirable. In addition, evaluate your current efforts on social media networks and possibly expand them, depending on your target audience. The World Bank, the UN Development Programme, and others offer workshops on the development and maintenance of platforms for communities of practice and on the design of mobile knowledge-sharing systems.

9.2.3   Capture experiences

Documenting some highly relevant experiences early on in the process will be helpful. It will demonstrate a fundamental process of the envisioned knowledge-sharing program—the conversion of experiential knowledge to explicit knowledge that can be further disseminated and shared. A good option for capturing experiences within the organization, if feasible, is to choose champions in your organization who may soon retire and have them share concrete advice on important solutions for the organization. For capturing external experiences, pick lessons learned from local experiences that merit urgent replication and scale up.

9.2.4   Implement the knowledge-sharing pilots

In the early days of executing the program, much of the energy will be devoted to demonstrating the value it provides. Swiftly implementing the pilots identified earlier is the ideal means of doing that.

These pilots can form the foundation for the remaining steps, providing the basis for some initial learning offerings, for measuring outcomes, and for scaling up.

Don't worry if everything is not yet perfect; after all, the pilots are still a learning experience for the knowledge-sharing coordination team and everyone involved. But put a strong effort into delivering the pilots, as senior management and some of the skeptics will be watching. Where possible, choose some "low-hanging fruit"—knowledge-sharing opportunities that are easy and ripe for the picking.

9.2.5   Develop learning offerings

Think about what your organization is doing in its ongoing learning areas, such as onboarding of new staff, technical skills development of experts, and management training. Check whether the current training efforts truly cater to their respective audiences, both in terms of the content and its delivery:

- » Are workshops and trainings mainly based on "canned" theories and international examples or do they use locally relevant cases?
- » Are the learning offerings largely lecture-based or are they participatory and learner-centric?

Ideally, you will be able to use the fruits of knowledge capturing in developing new offerings in the ongoing learning areas of your organization.

9.2.6   Measure outcomes

It is time to use the success measures defined earlier (section 9.1.6) to guide the collection of data and feedback on the knowledge capturing and sharing undertaken so far. If possible, compare the results to a baseline to demonstrate the value added. For example,

- » For internal knowledge sharing, show how it helped speed up or improve the quality of certain service delivery processes.
- » For external knowledge sharing, point to solutions that were adapted and replicated elsewhere thanks to the program.

9.2.7   Scale up

Knowledge sharing should not stop with a successful pilot. Now the real work is just about to start: making use of the positive momentum for the knowledge-sharing program by scaling it up. Scale up internally to get more departments excited and involved, and scale up externally to adapt and replicate tested solutions throughout the country and beyond.

APPENDIXES

A. Tools for Developing Knowledge-Sharing Strategies

1. Template for a Knowledge-Sharing Strategy Framework

2. Quality Checklist for a Knowledge-Sharing Framework

3. Example: Knowledge-Sharing Framework Document, Shanghai National Accounting Institute and Asia-Pacific Finance and Development Institute, China

B. Roles and Responsibilities: Functions and Terms of Reference

1. Knowledge-Sharing Steering Committee

2. Knowledge-Management/Knowledge-Sharing Coordination Team

3. Chief Knowledge and Learning Officer

4. Knowledge and Learning Specialist

5. Knowledge-Capturing Specialist

6. Audiovisual Media Specialist

7. Instructional Designer/Learning Designer

C. Knowledge Capturing

1. Example: Knowledge Asset, FMARD (Nigeria)

D. Knowledge-Sharing Tools and Templates

1. Overview: Knowledge-Sharing Instruments and Activities

2. Knowledge-Sharing Activity:

    a. Planning Questionnaire

    b. Implementation Checklist

    c. Evaluation Form

    d. Follow-Up Questionnaire

3. Template for After-Action Review Report

A. Tools for Developing Knowledge-Sharing Strategies

1. Template for a Knowledge-Sharing Strategy Framework
2. Quality Checklist for a Knowledge-Sharing Framework
3. Example: Knowledge-Sharing Framework Document, Shanghai National Accounting Institute and Asia-Pacific Finance and Development Institute, China

A.1 Template for a knowledge-sharing strategy framework

Chapter	Description	Examples
Introduction	Provide context and background. Why is knowledge sharing needed?	Increase service delivery effectiveness, address impact of high staff turnover, improve quality of solutions and innovation, take solutions to scale.
Stakeholders	List all relevant stakeholders and their needs for knowledge sharing.	Internal and external stakeholders, management, frontline teams, administrative functions, experts, new staff, partners, clients, local government counterparts, civil society, academia, private sector, international partners.
Knowledge-sharing principles	Describe the underlying guiding principles for successful knowledge sharing in your organization.	Relevance, practicality, timeliness, quality, accessibility, openness, inclusiveness, neutrality.
Vision, purpose, objectives	Describe the vision and goals. What can knowledge sharing do for the organization? How does it link to the overall mission of the organization?	Help deliver more effectively on mandate, establish organization as internationally recognized center of excellence/knowledge hub.
Internal knowledge-sharing • Leadership • Motivation • Internal knowledge flows • Platforms	Describe the role of senior management as leaders for knowledge sharing. Lay out specific motivators and incentives for knowledge sharing. Describe how the organization intends to increase knowledge flows across formal boundaries. Describe which existing and new platforms support knowledge sharing.	Act as role model, promote through communications and rhetoric, embed in vision and strategy, link closely to core business and operations, identify champions. Career development, visibility of contributors, formal recognition and awards, informal recognition by peers and supervisors, performance reviews, learning opportunities, and external visibility. Regular meetings, townhalls, organization-wide knowledge-sharing activities such as brown-bag lunches, cross-departmental sharing opportunities, team retreats, informal knowledge-sharing opportunities, provision of open spaces, extracurricular activities. Intranets, online platforms, database systems, knowledge repositories, process support services, expertise locator, social media platforms, e-mail, mobile systems.

Chapter	Description	Examples
External knowledge sharing		
• Brokering	External knowledge sharing can be divided into domestic and international dimensions, depending on the strategic positioning of the organization.	Brokering platform, mapping of knowledge supply and demand, proactive versus pull-brokering; use of international partners, academia, and thematic networks for brokering.
• External knowledge flows	Describe how knowledge recipients and providers can be matched and brought together, domestically and/or internationally.	Conferences, expert visits, knowledge fairs, study tours, workshops, multistakeholder dialogues, twinning arrangements, communities of practice.
• Platforms	Describe options for knowledge-sharing activities and programs to develop capabilities and scale up ideas and solutions. Describe which platforms the organization uses.	Domestically: online platforms, database systems, knowledge repositories, process support services, expertise locator, social media platforms, e-mail, mobile systems. Internationally: conferences, social media networks, sectoral networks, communities of practice, multilateral organizations.
Knowledge-sharing capabilities		
• Knowledge identification	Describe how relevant experiences and know-how gets identified in your organization.	Definition of identification criteria, organization of focus groups, interviews, peer learning events, work program reviews, surveys and questionnaires, expert locators.
• Knowledge capturing	Describe which skills, capabilities, and processes are needed for systematic capturing of experiences and lessons learned.	Knowledge assets and lessons learned notes, exit interviews, back-to-office reports, focus groups, surveys, polls.
• Validation	Describe the validation functions the organization will use to ensure consistency and high quality of knowledge and learning products.	Criteria, processes, and teams.
• Learning	Describe the future learning environment in your organization. What should learning look like and what will the organization do to provide its management and staff with the right technical and adaptive skills?	Use of local experiences in induction programs, technical training, workshops; use of internal experts and client stories; participatory and learner-centric approaches to learning.
• Sharing	Describe the skills needed to ensure that collaboration and the flow of knowledge are improved in the organization.	Skills to anchor, define, design, implement, and follow up on knowledge-sharing programs and activities.
• Monitoring and evaluation	Describe how knowledge-sharing efforts will be monitored and results measured.	Quality standards. *Type of evaluation:* positive deviance, participatory evaluation, horizontal evaluation. *Data collection:* balanced scorecard, questionnaires, retrospective outcome assessment, web-based surveys, most-significant change, before- and after-action reviews, opinion polls, diaries. *Techniques for analysis:* cost-benefit, cost-effectiveness, numeric weighting.

Chapter	Description	Examples
Partnerships	Describe existing and potential future partnerships:	
• Knowledge partnerships	To improve know-how and to connect to potential recipients of knowledge.	Thematic networks, communities of practice, partnerships with academia, peers, bilateral and multilateral development organizations, twinning arrangements.
• Functional partnerships	To support knowledge and learning functions, for example through outsourcing.	Outsourcing of knowledge functions such as capturing/documentation, event organization, learning offering development, knowledge-sharing program implementation, facilitation, IT platform hosting and administration.
• Financing partnerships	To access financial resources to support knowledge sharing.	Bilateral collaborations, bilateral and multilateral development organizations, academia, foundations, trust funds, public-private partnerships, private sector, crowd-funding, sponsorship arrangements.
Core functions and governance	Describe how knowledge sharing will be anchored in the organization and define roles and responsibilities. In some cases these can be complemented by specific definitions of functions and job descriptions. Clarify how knowledge and learning can become everyone's responsibility.	*Functions:* chief knowledge and learning officer, knowledge-sharing steering committee, knowledge-sharing coordination team, departmental knowledge and learning officers. *Roles:* journalist, analyst, editor, librarian, facilitator, broker, instructional designer, communication expert, communities of practice manager, IT specialist.

A.2 Quality checklist for a knowledge-sharing framework

The proposed guideline in the framework document . . .

1. Is clearly guided by the mission, values, and strategies of our organization:

   ☐ Yes
   ☐ No   *If No, proposed change:*

2. Has a clear statement of purpose, value, and importance to our organization:

   ☐ Yes
   ☐ No   *If No, proposed change:*

3. Provides sufficient guidance for the development of procedures and guidelines that lead to practical implementation:

   ☐ Yes
   ☐ No   *If No, proposed change:*

4. Communicates lines of accountability to the leadership of our organization:

   ☐ Yes
   ☐ No   *If No, proposed change:*

5. Is appropriate to our current conditions and objectives:

   ☐ Yes
   ☐ No   *If No, proposed change:*

6. Is feasible to implement:

   ☐ Yes
   ☐ No   *If No, proposed change:*

A.3 Example: Knowledge-sharing framework document, Shanghai National Accounting Institute and Asia-Pacific Finance and Development Institute, China[1]

Strategic Framework for Knowledge Sharing

Draft for exemplary purposes

ASIA-PACIFIC FINANCE AND DEVELOPMENT INSTITUTE

CONTENTS

1. Introduction

2. Vision, Purpose, Objectives

3. SNAI/AFDI Knowledge-Sharing Principles

4. Internal Knowledge Sharing

5. Domestic Knowledge Sharing

6. International Knowledge Sharing

7. Governance

1. Introduction

   1.1 The Asia-Pacific Finance and Development Institute (AFDI) is a public institution under the administration of the Ministry of Finance, China, established in order to continue China's contribution to institutional capacity building in the Asia-Pacific region. The establishment of AFDI not only signifies regularization of the efforts of Chinese government in capacity building for the international community, but also the expansion of the target area to be covered by the efforts of Chinese government. In addition to the APEC mechanism, AFDI has also worked with ASEAN+3, Forum for East Asia and Latin America Cooperation (FEALAC) and many other organizations.

---

[1] This document is informed by a self-assessment by selected staff during the December 2015 workshop "Getting Ready for Knowledge-Sharing: Self-Assessment, Visioning, and Planning," supported by the Leadership, Learning, and Innovation Vice-Presidency of the World Bank. The framework has been developed as part of the 100-day action plan to support a more systematic approach to knowledge sharing.

1.2 The Shanghai National Accounting Institute (SNAI) is a public service institution affiliated to the Ministry of Finance of China. SNAI also hosts AFDI. In the past 10-plus years, SNAI has sought to find pedagogy proper for senior financial and accounting professionals, cultivate high-end talent for the accounting industry and provide advanced continuing education for macroeconomic regulators, large-and-medium-sized SOEs, financial institutions and intermediaries. Today, SNAI has created its own unique teaching philosophy and methods underpinned by the three pillars of degree education, executive development program and distance education.

1.3 Learning is at the heart of both SNAI and AFDI: two entities that are strongly interconnected. Within the organization, SNAI/AFDI aims to optimize operational processes to become more effective in all areas of their work program and mandate, including more systematical capture and sharing of critical lessons and experiences. In China and internationally the organizations jointly can position itself as a knowledge center sharing valuable experiences on accounting and public sector finance and promote systematic knowledge sharing and knowledge-sharing approaches among stakeholders.

2. Vision, Purpose, Objectives

2.1 SNAI/AFDI strives to become a knowledge hub in the finance sector in China and beyond by 2020 to scale up successful practices and promote knowledge sharing.

2.2 The purpose of this strategic framework for knowledge-sharing is to put in place a clear policy framework that will underpin and guide the knowledge-sharing activities based on the vision and the objectives.

2.3 In order for SNAI/AFDI to achieve its vision, it must address knowledge sharing at three levels: internal to the organization, domestically with its partners and stakeholders across China, and internationally via South-South knowledge exchange.

2.4 Organizational capabilities of SNAI/AFDI are considered critical to sustain effective knowledge sharing. These critical capacity areas all get attention in this Framework Document and cover eight interconnected domains. Four of these domains relate more to the enabling environment for knowledge sharing and four of them more to the technical capabilities that are deemed critical for knowledge sharing.

3. SNAI/AFDI Knowledge-Sharing Principles

3.1 SNAI/AFDI knowledge represents value—it is the basis for high quality learning and can foster great inspiration and innovation inside and outside the organization. The organization therefore encourages the introduction, use and development of instruments and approaches for improved knowledge capturing, documenting, sharing and learning within and between its departments, and more broadly throughout and beyond the organizational boundaries.

3.2 SNAI/AFDI regards knowledge sharing (KS) as a critical component of its operational culture and work ethic. Although KS activities are often voluntary by nature, the organization will put in place specific mechanisms to further incentivize and reward KS behavior at individual as well as group/team level. It may also establish minimal standards for all employees to meet.

3.3 SNAI/AFDI knowledge should be accessible to a wide audience of learners and where possible open to feedback and revision. The organization recognizes the importance of information and communication technology in support of this, especially in facilitating learning and exchange of knowledge across geographical distances, and invests in its development in accordance with the needs of the participants and users.

3.4 SNAI/AFDI knowledge and knowledge products should be Quality Assured for multiple aspects, including:

» **Relevance.** Not everything in the organization needs to be captured. Relevance relates to the extent to which information or experiences can help individuals or teams to operate more effectively and/or replicate solutions.

» **Timeliness** is another dimension of relevance. The organization should strive to capture knowledge when it matters most to others and clearly monitor different versions of explicit knowledge products over time.

» **Professional and methodological rigor and completeness.** Completeness refers to a pre-defined set of topics that need to be part of every knowledge product. This can include the name of the author and for example metatags for search engines. Professional and methodological rigor refers to clear referencing to sources and the overall logic and quality of the reasoning.

» **Legal compliance and confidentiality.** Knowledge captured for sharing obviously should always be within the legal domain (including copy right) and also the ethical domain of the organization. It should furthermore be clear if these documents are open to all or have restricted parts of information, for instance because they have sensitive information about individuals or company specifics.

» **Accessibility** refers to making the knowledge available and searchable in an easy manner to a range of audiences through on- or offline mechanisms.

3.5 SNAI/AFDI knowledge has value that reaches beyond theoretical value—for learning—but also has practical value for implementation and/or replication.

4. Internal Knowledge Sharing

Within the organization SNAI/AFDI aims to optimize operational processes to become more effective in all areas of their work program and mandate, including more systematic capture and sharing of critical lessons and experiences. In addition, AFDI/SNAI experienced the power of more participatory approaches, which could complement and add significantly to the existing pedagogies for training students. Making students part of new and innovative learning trajectories and approaches will become a bigger part of daily teaching and could bring competitive advantages for the organization.

4.1 Enabling Environment

SNAI/AFDI believes that a strong knowledge-sharing **culture** is vital for the organization to thrive and deliver on its mandate. It will help to better collaborate across teams and departments, increase efficiencies of staff, help foster innovation and improve scale up of good practices in all areas of work of the organization. SNAI/AFDI will therefore expand its efforts to foster such a culture in which knowledge sharing becomes everybody's business. A number of concrete practices will be established that motivate and incentivize staff at all levels to become knowledge-sharing champions.

Senior management empowers all staff to become active knowledge sharers by creating an open environment where everybody's opinion counts and experience is valued as contribution to the continuous improving of the service delivery effectiveness of the organization. Senior management will serve as a role model for continuous and effective knowledge sharing.

SNAI/AFDI fosters internal knowledge sharing and cross-departmental collaboration through a set of **motivators** that will ensure knowledge sharing will become everybody's business in the organization:

» **Career development:** A number of intrinsic incentives are discussed with staff which include personal growth opportunities, new career path opportunities that relate to knowledge management and knowledge sharing, and expanded roles of facilitators of learning offerings.

» **Job descriptions:** SNAI/AFDI will consider including knowledge sharing in the job descriptions of all staff. Knowledge sharing thus becomes a critical part of day-to-day work of staff which will help increase personal performance, team work and collaboration across organizational boundaries.

» **Credit to contributors of knowledge products:** SNAI/AFDI recognizes the efforts of staff in contributing to knowledge products by ensuring they are adequately mentioned as authors, editors or contributors.

» **Knowledge-sharing awards and formal recognition:** SNAI/AFDI recognizes outstanding knowledge-sharing performance of staff through a knowledge-sharing award that will be issued on a yearly basis. The award will be given to teams that demonstrate exceptional knowledge-sharing behavior. The award will be tied to modest funds that will be provided to the team.

» **Informal recognition by supervisors:** Senior- and mid-level management of the organization recognize good knowledge-sharing performance through informal conversations or emails that demonstrate that the organization is taking note of the knowledge-sharing contribution of the staff.

» **Knowledge contributions showcase and peer rating:** SNAI/AFDI showcases contributions to the knowledge pool that receive exceptional feedback and ratings, for example on the knowledge-sharing platform.

» **Performance review:** SNAI/AFDI takes note of lacking knowledge-sharing behavior in the annual performance review of staff. All staff will be evaluated along a clear set of measurable indicators as they relate to knowledge sharing.

» **Training opportunities:** The institute rewards staff who demonstrate outstanding knowledge-sharing behavior through provision of access to additional attractive training offerings.

Knowledge Platforms and Repositories. Existing Platforms, tools and Repositories (including Intranet, Work Tile, WeChat) exist in SNAI/AFDI and can be further leveraged on for organization-wide knowledge sharing and serve as internal content management and information-sharing spaces. The main internal knowledge platform function is to share information within the organization and facilitate knowledge sharing among staff. The intranet platform will need to be further assessed for its ability to fully support capturing, managing, sharing and finding (search) of valuable expertise and experiences.

Mechanisms that support knowledge sharing. There are different means and mechanisms in SNAI/AFDI in support of knowledge capture, which can be further utilized, including:

» Regular face to face meetings—SNAI/AFDI has a regular meeting platform for individuals who want to share experience with one another and using proven techniques such as After Action Reviews (AAR) and peer assists. A set of questions will be developed to identify and capture the experience, focusing on the "how". This knowledge/experience should be based on a concrete problem/challenge and explain how the problem was solved with concrete actions taken, the results achieved and any particular lessons to be learned from the experience. Each template will also contain a section on recommendations.

» Website platform—SNAI/AFDI will create a social knowledge platform gathering in one place courses, books, videos, news and courses that match the users' interests. It also helps users build their profiles that express their skills and area of expertise.

» WeChat platform—SNAI/AFDI has created (and further leverage) WeChat groups for different groups and functional teams. WeChat is a means to promote two-way sharing among individuals, teams and organizational-wide staff including all administrative, finance, human resources, and teaching staff.

» Email platform—SNAI/AFDI existing email system is one of the most commonly used communication tools in its operation's environment, increasing the speed and ease with which information can be shared by staff across the globe. However, the organization needs to establish a company-wide policy on bulk unsolicited or 'spam' emails, together with a policy of deleting spam emails without responding.

» Mobile Platform—SNAI/AFDI acknowledges the ubiquity of smart phones in today's society and will create a mobile experience solutions finder. This solutions finder is innovative in that it can be used on the go in virtually any venue.

Flow of knowledge between departments. SNAI/AFDI is aware that institutional knowledge could flow more and better between and across departments and not just top-down. Options, such as job rotation and secondments, to improve flow will be further explored so that good practices in one department can be shared with other departments. Formal and informal instruments will be considered to support optimal knowledge flows, including templates for (overseas) study trip reports and brown back lunches to share what has been learned in trainings.

4.2   Technical Skills

Knowledge Capture. Capturing knowledge is considered valuable to the organization in various ways, including: recognizing good practices that can be replicated across teams and departments; building alignment between corporate and teams strategic direction; gaining greater efficiency by minimizing repeated mistakes and reducing the need to reinvent the wheel; pushing for a more sustainable service in support of the strategic plan; and retaining leaving staff's skills and customer relationship expertise.

SNAI/AFDI recognizes therefore that it has important knowledge that deserves to be captured well, including on:

» Staff expertise—knowing different individuals' profile, expertise, and background;

» Internal customer relationships—how to identify and work for different departments;

» Resources—knowledge of available resources and how to acquire and leverage these;

» Work Processes—systematic processes with clear roles and responsibilities;

Editing Knowledge Products. Knowledge can change rapidly. A practice that SNAI/AFDI intends to enhance is the ability for staff to comment and add easily to existing pieces of knowledge and information, pose comments or questions or edit content.

Quality Assurance of Knowledge Products. Validation of knowledge products requires dedicated attention before it is shared; including for whom it will be accessible, which can exceed department boundaries. SNAI/AFDI knowledge and knowledge products should be Quality Assured for multiple aspects, including:

» **Relevance.** Not everything in the organization needs to be captured. Relevance relates to the extent to which information or experiences can help individuals or teams to operate more effectively and/or replicate solutions.

» **Timeliness** is another dimension of relevance. The organization should strive to capture knowledge when it matters most to others and clearly monitor different versions of explicit knowledge products over time.

» **Professional and methodological Rigor and Completeness.** Completeness refers to a pre-defined set of topics that need to be part of every knowledge product. This can include the name of the author and for example metatags for search engines. Professional and methodological rigor refers to clear referencing to sources and the overall logic and quality of the reasoning.

» **Legal compliance and confidentiality.** Knowledge captured for sharing obviously should always be within the legal domain (including copy right) and also the ethical domain of the organization. It should furthermore be clear if these documents are open to all or have restricted parts of information, for instance because they have sensitive information about individuals or company specifics.

» **Accessibility** refers to making the knowledge available and searchable in an easy manner to a range of audiences through on- or offline mechanisms.

To refine its Quality Assurance process the organization will further consider a number of options, including:

> » **Asking experts.** SNAI/AFDI needs to establish a mechanism to systematically inquire whether the knowledge is reliable to share. In some cases, outside experts of the same domain should be consulted to get opinions on that knowledge. Besides having evaluation forms, SNAI/AFDI should establish a mechanism to organize and facilitate focus groups to verify the truthfulness of the knowledge captured.

> » **DO'S and DON'TS list.** SNAI/AFDI provides a clear do's and don'ts list with specific examples. The key is a solid foundation set by unified policies that can guide standards and procedures to both minimize risk and comply with regulations now and in the future. Concrete examples will support that.

Sharing and disseminating knowledge will be improved through introducing a number of elements:

> » **Test environment.** SNAI/AFDI should provide a premise that allows staff to learn, try-out (pilot), implement and review–giving the opportunity to try out, successful or not.

> » **Action Learning.** Some departments already require staff to learn (in parts) through actual work. Action learning should be promoted in all departments.

> » **Bite size learning.** Some traditional learning offerings can be turned into bite-sized chunks. Bite-size sessions are generally held on-line, eliminating the challenges that arise from taking employees to a venue; transport, meals and high costs. Bite-size sessions are also good for mobile access and integration.

> » **Best Practices.** The organization establishes a process to identify and share best practices among teams and individuals. It will be critical to review best practices over time.

> » **Online sharing practices.** Various documents and tools are available in the organization online, including for example news bulletins, internal procedures and other knowledge aimed at improving efficiency and effectiveness; interactive platforms and FAQs. SNAI/AFDI further considers more moderated discussions and lectures and special interest communities of practice, such as book clubs, and more use of social media to support online training courses.

Knowledge-Sharing Evaluation: managers and heads of departments are naturally positioned to monitor and evaluate individual staff members' contribution to knowledge sharing as part of their formal appraisal and coaching of staff.

Training Evaluation: significant attention is given by SNAI/AFDI to evaluate how students perceive trainings, but less attention is paid to internally act upon feedback and incorporate changes and improvements to the trainings.

Impact Evaluation: tracer studies could be considered to further assess what students do with their newly gained knowledge after they leave the classroom. Online spaces for alumni may support this function and are already being used and will be considered at larger scale.

5. Domestic Knowledge Sharing

Domestically SNAI/AFDI has the objective to not only grow its capacity in Organizational Knowledge Sharing, but to also teach others in the approach and share best practices countrywide, among others through an Annual Forum at the China Knowledge Sharing Center (CKSC) where leading institutions share good practices and connect practitioners and subject matter experts.

5.1 Enabling Environment

SNAI/AFDI recognizes domestic knowledge sharing as a critical contributor to the effective service delivery of the organization.

Official mandate: SNAI/AFDI seeks to get the official mandate to become a hub for knowledge sharing on finance and accounting. Such a mandate will provide the necessary enabling environment for this important role. Senior management will thus seek approval for this mandate with the Ministry of Finance in China.

Leadership support for capacity development on organizational knowledge sharing: SNAI/AFDI promotes and develops the capacity of other organizations working on finance and accounting in China to become knowledge-sharing organizations, using the World Bank framework and approach to organizational knowledge-sharing capability development. The organization institutes a team to deliver this program to partner institutions across China.

Integration of local experience in learning: the organization further invests in the integration of practical knowledge and experiences in the learning offerings of the organization. In order to better cater to the needs of counterparts and clients, it will design learning offerings in such a way as to meet their specific learning needs and provide concrete examples of actual solutions that were captured in China.

Communication: SNAI/AFDI demonstrates leadership on knowledge sharing by actively promoting and communicating about the merits of open knowledge sharing and exchange of experiences on finance and accounting with domestic counterparts and partners.

Brokering role for finance and accounting experiences: SNAI/AFDI plays the role of an honest broker of experience and solutions to pertinent challenges on finance and accounting across all provinces in China. The organization develops dedicated knowledge-sharing opportunities and events that allow for the systematic sharing of experience such as forums, web discussions and events.

Recognition: SNAI/AFDI recognizes special knowledge-sharing efforts of local finance authorities and partner institutions at the sub-national level through a special award, certificate or trophy. To incentivize individuals it will also offer the opportunity of knowledge-sharing champions to become mentors, resource persons and secondees for knowledge sharing in the organization.

Partnerships: SNAI/AFDI strives to ever expand efforts on developing meaningful partnerships with partners across China to foster effective delivery of high quality services and learning. The organization recognizes that such partnerships are essential for the effective development of a rich pool of knowledge on finance and accounting in China and the brokering of such across domestic partners and local constituents.

The organization believes partnerships are critical at three levels: Content/capturing, Implementation and Finance.

Partnerships on content and capturing of experiences

» **Partnerships with finance and accounting peer institutes:** SNAI/AFDI will seek even closer ties and collaboration among the three national accounting institutes in China and further reach out to peer institutes to elevate cooperation and joint learning on mutually relevant topics.

» **Experience capturing:** The organization develops powerful partnerships with institutions across China to effectively capture and document relevant experiences on finance and accounting across China.

Partnerships on Implementation

» **Event logistics:** The organization stands ready to serve as a competent partner for the provision of logistics and event management services across China.

» **Technology partnerships:** In order to effectively conduct high quality knowledge-sharing activities, SNAI/AFDI recognize the importance of technology and therefore develop and further foster existing partnerships with technology providers.

Partnerships on Finance

» **Finance partnerships:** SNAI/AFDI seek partners, for example from the private sector, who can actively contribute to our knowledge-sharing efforts, either through in-kind contributions, reduced costs or financial contributions.

A central knowledge-sharing budget: The organization recognizes that funding is critical to effectively becoming a knowledge-sharing organization. SNAI/AFDI therefore will develop a dedicated knowledge-sharing budget to foster knowledge sharing on finance and accounting practices and solutions across China. In the short term some reallocation of existing budgets will be undertaken to accommodate the funding needs of urgent activities. The budget will include provisions for staffing, systems infrastructure and dedicated knowledge capturing and sharing activities. The latter may include study tours, exchange programs, participation in networks, and related travel.

Additional funding sources: SNAI/AFDI may seek additional funding on knowledge sharing from private sector partners.

Capacity development support for KS budget development: SNAI/AFDI supports the development process of local partners to develop dedicated budgets for knowledge sharing.

Mechanisms that will be put to use in support of domestic knowledge sharing in China are:

» **Free Website:** The (free) portal website for Chinese accountants can be further leveraged on. It already provides news and relevant info for accountants and the organization aims to increase the number of active visitors as well as its influence through facilitated discussions.

» **Fee-for-service Website:** The existing E-learning platform, which is a charged service, could further benefit from integrating OKS components and approaches–which will be further explored.

» A so-called **"Open classroom"** is organized in different cities and a Forum at the SNAI facility.

» A **SNAI/AFDI OKS course** will be further considered for delivery to Chinese counterparts and may be tested in a pilot form.

5.2 Technical Skills

The core competitiveness of an organization lies in the capability of its staff and good team spirit within the organization. Therefore, SNAI/AFDI has worked on enhancing its own capacity building while serving to strengthen capacity building in areas of finance and development for the region.

There is still substantial space for the organization to strengthen its capacity including capacity to identify demand, to integrate resources, and to organize activities more efficiently and effectively.

Increased capabilities will help maintain competitive advantage and improve capability in order to become a premier and reputable knowledge-sharing organization in China. With rapidly growing competition, true knowledge-sharing capability can provide the organization with a competitive edge.

Learning from good practices outside SNAI/AFDI. The organization believes strongly in development of its staff and allocates specific funding to encourage staff to participate in trainings, knowledge sharing, and other capacity building programs. For internal learning, SNAI/AFDI will make a conscious effort to tap into good practices that exist outside the organization on a continuous basis and broker some of these good practices as well.

Such good practices and lessons can cover a wide range of topics and initiatives such as:

» The ability to re-structure and re-allocate resources

» Marketing and sales capability

» Innovation, creativity and responsiveness

» Partnership management

» Benchmarking practices

» Customer relationship management focusing on campaign planning, customer services and (big data) analytics

» Establish a profitable and sustainable business model

» Strengthen and strategize human resources management

Launching a knowledge hub will require attention across various dimensions:

» Organize regular sessions for knowledge sharing, exchange visits, research, projects

» Act as a third party to provide platform for multi-dimension of partners to display their valuable experience

» Leverage official channels to release important information

» Provide a knowledge-sharing platform for arranging forums, salons (simulation platform for internal training) and lectures

Validation of Domestic Knowledge Products. The domestic knowledge-sharing validation criteria are similar to those for internal knowledge sharing:

» Relevance

» Timeliness

» Professional and methodological Rigor and Completeness

» Legal compliance and confidentiality

» Accessibility

Localizing solutions. SNAI/AFDI strives to better integrate **practical (local)** experiences in learning offerings to support scale up of solutions to critical challenges. They will explore to this end:

» Organization internal training

» Institutional research, interviews

Sharing solutions. SNAI/AFDI aims to engage stakeholders in a more participatory way through strategically selecting competitors/customers to become partners, and through a platform for multiple stakeholders to share experiences and processes and set industry standards.

SNAI/AFDI has set out to develop a strong **monitoring and evaluation framework** to assess the effectiveness of its domestic knowledge-sharing work. Currently it monitors some programs better than others. Strengthening such a system will be an important area of work.

6. International Knowledge Sharing

SNAI/AFDI sees substantial opportunities to become a knowledge hub in the Asia Pacific region, and key partner and information center (database) in Asia Pacific for relevant experience and knowledge in finance and accounting. Building blocks for the knowledge hub are:

» International KS best practices

» Summit/Forum of international knowledge-sharing institutions

» International KS database (experience and information)

» An exchange platform

6.1   Enabling Environment

SNAI/AFDI regards international knowledge sharing as a fundamental pillar to its work as it enriches programs with latest international best practice solutions, as well as provides the opportunity for the organization to share expertise on finance and accounting with international partners and peers.

SNAI/AFDI strives to share China's experience on finance and accounting in such a way that it helps international peers, both in the Asia-Pacific region and beyond, to solve their particular development challenges. The organization wants to increase long-term partnerships and twinning arrangements, following the positive experience with the national leading accounting professionals program ("Top CFO") at the domestic level.

SNAI/AFDI therefore strives to develop an Asia-Pacific Knowledge-sharing Center (AKSC) which promotes knowledge sharing among the countries in the Asia-Pacific region. The program would act as a broker of China's finance and accounting expertise to international partners.

The knowledge-sharing efforts are not for profit but strive to be **cost recovering** through a fee-for-service model in which costs for videoconference, logistics, venues and staff, spending for participants from developing countries, are covered by SNAI/AFDI, while the partner organization cover travel and accommodation for study tours, unless the program costs are covered by third party sponsors.

System and platforms of the organization will be assessed in more details for its ability to support international knowledge sharing. There are various systems and platforms currently in use. Systems include:

- » Wechat, email system
- » Library system
- » Information management system of international graduate students
- » Office Automation system
- » GDLN website and database
- » Knowledge hub community

Platforms include:

- » All the above systems
- » Joint school programs
- » Forums jointly organized with partners
- » Accountants' Vision website
- » Online courses
- » Visiting Scholar programs

Leverage through partnerships. A specific partnership strategy will be developed in support of the international KS ambition of the organization. To this end both existing and new partners will be considered. Currently SNAI/AFDI has several partnerships, including:

» International Financial and Development Institutions, such as the World Bank (WB), the Asian Development Bank (ADB), the International Monetary Fund (IMF), the Organization for Economic Co-operation and Development (OECD), the International Fund for Agriculture Development (IFAD);

» Professional Accounting bodies, such as the Chinese Institute of Certified Public Accountants (CICPA), the Association of Chartered Certified Accountants (ACCA), the Chartered Institute of Management Accountants (CIMA), the Institute of Chartered Accountants in England and Wales (ICAEW), the Institute of Management Accountants (IMA), the Australian Society of Certified Practicing Accountants (CPA Australia), the Certified General Accountants Association of Canada (CGA-Canada), the Extensible Business Reporting Language International consortium (the XBRL International);

» Universities, such as the Chinese University of Hong Kong (CUHK), the Arizona State University (ASU), the Korea Development Institute School of Public Policy and Management (KDI School);

» Government Affiliated Institutions, such as the Institute of Financial Training (IFT) of Ministry of Finance, Vietnam; the Economics and Finance Institute (EFI) of Ministry Of Economy and Finance, Cambodia.

6.2 Technical Skills

Monitoring and Evaluation. SNAI/AFDI actively partners with leading organizations around the world in various forms and shapes. Examples include MoUs with the governments of Vietnam and Myanmar, with KDI School in Korea and through the GDLN network for example.

Monitoring and Evaluation of programs is considered important and takes place in different ways. For example the EMBA with Arizona University is ranked highly in the Financial Times ranking which is a helpful indicator for the success of the program.

While partnerships and joint programs prove valuable for knowledge exchange, SNAI/AFDI recognizes that sharpening and detailing the specific objectives of these knowledge exchanges and programs is crucial and support also improved monitoring and evaluation efforts. Knowledge collaborations and exchanges at times lack a detailed set of objectives and therefore cannot be monitored in a rigid manner nor can they be evaluated effectively.

International training programs such as the 2-year Master's program in China for participants from developing countries may offer huge potential for integrating some of the OKS learning pedagogy; both online and offline.

7. Governance

SNAI/AFDI recognizes the importance of creating a knowledge-sharing culture where all staff have a certain responsibility and role to play. It is not the work of one person or department, but integrated in job descriptions for all staff, including technical and support functions.

To fully implement the KS vision and objectives, a solid governance structure for organizational knowledge sharing at internal, domestic and international level will be put in place.

Currently a task team has been formed and for Team Members, Coordinators and the Head of the 100-Day Task Team, Terms of References are being detailed along the following lines:

Team Members

- » Complete assigned tasks on time
- » Report assigned task status periodically
- » Share work results regularly
- » Being a role model for others (not OKS members)

Coordinators

- » Communicate clearly
- » Assign tasks to relevant members effectively
- » Follow up and report milestones
- » While unexpected event happens, provide solution collaboratively

100-Day Plan Team Head

- » Develop tasks and assign tasks to member accordingly
- » Provide clear deadline for each task
- » Make decision promptly
- » Monitor progress
- » Report to institute leader on issues and communicate clearly back to members

B. Roles and Responsibilities: Functions and Terms of Reference

1. Knowledge-Sharing Steering Committee

2. Knowledge-Management/Knowledge-Sharing Coordination Team

3. Chief Knowledge and Learning Officer

4. Knowledge and Learning Specialist

5. Knowledge-Capturing Specialist

6. Audiovisual Media Specialist

7. Instructional/Learning Designer

B.1 Knowledge-sharing steering committee

Description

This document sets the Terms of Reference for [Your Organization's] Knowledge-Sharing Steering Committee. The Terms of Reference establish the Steering Committee's mission, objectives, membership, and operational procedures. The Knowledge Sharing Steering Committee is the governing body for guiding the development, implementation, and continuous improvement of [Your Organization's] knowledge-sharing initiatives, policies, and strategy.

(Use this section to provide background information related to the establishment of the Steering Committee, its mission, and objectives. This will include decisions made regarding knowledge sharing in your organization, relevant events, related organizational structures and hierarchies, and the process behind the establishment of the committee.)

Responsibilities

» Devising a strategy for knowledge sharing

» Supervising the knowledge-sharing change process

» Creating a broad, organization-wide awareness of the policies, perspectives, and goals associated with all knowledge-sharing activities

» Ensuring that the roles and responsibilities for the performance of the knowledge-sharing programs are clear and complementary

» Fostering communications and cooperation across business units and departments for knowledge-sharing programs, policies, and activities and ensuring alignment of operational units with support functions in their implementation of knowledge sharing

» Establishing performance measures and metrics for the organization's knowledge-sharing activities

» Appointing an implementation team and its leader

» Approving knowledge-sharing partnerships

» Supporting and regularly briefing senior management on all knowledge-sharing issues

(Use this section to describe the specific roles and responsibilities of the Knowledge Sharing Steering Committee members. This will include the activities that they will be accountable for, what their commitments are and the expectations of each member of the Knowledge Sharing Steering Committee.)

Qualifications/Membership

(Use this section to list the members of the Knowledge Sharing Steering Committee; include title as well as role within the team.)

Operations/Frequency of Meetings

(Use this section to establish the frequency of the Steering Committee's meetings and how these are to be conducted. Include how the decisions and minutes will be shared with staff.)

B.2   Knowledge-management/Knowledge-sharing coordination team

Description

This document sets the Terms of Reference for [Your Organization's] Knowledge-Management Coordination Team. The Terms of Reference establish the team's mission, objectives, membership and operational procedures. The Knowledge-Management Coordination Team is the implementing body for knowledge-sharing initiatives, policies, and strategy. The team is composed of knowledge and learning specialists and representatives from all operational and administrative departments of the organization. The team is in charge of implementation of major knowledge-sharing programs and activities in [Your Organization]; relevant events, platforms, and systems; development of knowledge and learning products and offerings; and other activities as they relate to the knowledge-sharing strategy framework. It further monitors the organization's knowledge-sharing activities and feeds performance reports back to the Knowledge Sharing Steering Committee.

(Use this section to provide any relevant background information related to the establishment of the team, its mission, and objectives.)

Responsibilities

» Implementation of the knowledge-sharing strategy

» Development of knowledge-sharing-related budgets

» Monitoring of knowledge-sharing-related expenses

» Coordination and organization of organization-wide and cross-departmental knowledge-sharing activities and events

- » Coordination of knowledge capturing efforts in the departments
- » Proactive development of innovative internal and external knowledge-sharing activities
- » Ensuring quality control and timely validation of knowledge assets
- » Coordination of the development of high-quality knowledge and learning products
- » Coordination of the design and implementation of high-quality learning offerings
- » Implementation and maintenance of knowledge-sharing systems and platforms
- » Design, implementation, and management of communities of practice and knowledge-sharing networks
- » Coordination of knowledge-sharing-related monitoring & evaluation and reporting efforts
- » Development of communications on knowledge-sharing-related activities
- » Implementation and active use of collaborations and partnerships as they relate to knowledge sharing and peer learning, including identification of outsourcing partners
- » Day-to-day liaison with domestic and international partners on knowledge-sharing activities

(Use this section to describe the specific roles and responsibilities of the Knowledge Management Coordination Team members. This will include the activities that they will be accountable for, their commitments, and the expectations of each team member.)

Qualifications/Membership

(Use this section to list each member of the Knowledge-Management Coordination Team; include title as well as role within the team.)

Operations/Frequency of Meetings

(Use this section to establish the frequency of the Knowledge-Management Coordination Team's meetings and how they are to be conducted. Include how decisions and minutes will be shared with staff.)

B.3   Chief knowledge and learning officer (CKO/CLO)

Job description

The Chief Knowledge and Learning Officer is part of the senior management team of the organization and oversees the design and implementation of the organization's knowledge management and learning strategies. The CKO/CLO develops efficiencies in the knowledge value chain by creating an enabling environment that is conducive to systematic knowledge sharing and organizational learning. He/she oversees the implementation of a knowledge infrastructure that supports informed decision making and continuous learning to prepare management and staff to deliver on their operational tasks in the most effective manner.

Responsibilities

» Oversee the development and implementation of a knowledge management strategy/framework/policies for the organization

» Oversee the development of functions, systems, tools, and processes that make use of knowledge to improve organizational effectiveness

» Actively promote the use of knowledge and learning within and outside the organization

» Be a role model for exemplary knowledge-sharing behavior to colleagues and partners of the organization

» Identify, promote, and use knowledge and learning partnerships that support and enrich knowledge management and sharing within and beyond the organization

» Encourage knowledge capturing and sharing throughout the organization

» Design and implement incentive mechanisms to reward exemplary knowledge capturing and sharing behavior

» Design and implement a results framework to monitor and evaluate effectiveness of knowledge and learning related measures

Qualifications

» A master's degree in knowledge management, instructional design, learning, or a related field and at least 10 years' applied experience in developing, managing, and implementing knowledge-management strategies

» Experience in organizational change management

» Excellent collaborative leadership skills

» Excellent interpersonal and people management skills, including the ability to motivate others

» Strong strategic-thinking and integration skills, with ability to identify opportunities and obstacles for systematic knowledge capturing and sharing within the organization

» Sound understanding of technologies, platforms, and IT infrastructure that facilitate knowledge management and sharing

» Good communication and listening skills

B.4   Knowledge and learning specialist

Job description

The Knowledge and Learning Specialist executes the knowledge and learning strategy of the organization and implements the knowledge and learning activities of the organization/department. The specialist sets up and manages knowledge management and learning systems and administers the infrastructure for systematic capturing, managing, sharing, and finding of information.

Responsibilities

- » Helps to foster organization-wide knowledge sharing, so that the organization's know-how, information, and experience is shared inside and, where applicable, outside the organization with partners and other stakeholders
- » Gathers and organizes information for the organization's knowledge repository
- » Facilitates seamless knowledge sharing across the organization's departments
- » Interacts regularly with operations colleagues to ensure continuous capturing, managing, and sharing of critical knowledge in the organization
- » Manages the content on the organization's knowledge and learning platforms
- » Analyzes the characteristics of existing and emerging technologies and their use for better management and sharing of knowledge
- » Develops the taxonomies of the organization's knowledge and learning repositories
- » Supports the design of the organization's knowledge and learning platforms and functionalities
- » Extracts high-value knowledge assets for dissemination
- » Supports the advocating, training, and mainstreaming of knowledge management and learning functions in the organization
- » Manages the organization's community-of-practice platforms
- » Models active knowledge sharing throughout the organization and with partners

Qualifications

- » A bachelor's degree in knowledge management, instructional design, learning, or a related field and at least five years' applied experience in setting up and administrating knowledge management and learning systems
- » Sound understanding of technologies, platforms, and IT infrastructure that facilitate knowledge management and sharing
- » Ability to develop an information architecture and taxonomies to support findability of the organization's knowledge assets
- » Good team work and collaboration skills
- » Good interpersonal skills and the ability to motivate others to contribute to and make use of the knowledge and learning offerings of the organization
- » Good communication and listening skills
- » Attention to detail

» Ability to quickly develop a sound understanding of the operational departments' knowledge needs and assets

» Ability to assess situations quickly and make independent decisions regarding capturing and sharing of knowledge assets

» Basic understanding of common business processes within the organization as well as with external partners

» Proactive work ethic

B.5   Knowledge-capturing specialist

Job description

The Knowledge-Capturing Specialist supports the organization-wide knowledge identification, capturing, validation, and formatting processes. The specialist extracts and documents valuable experiences and lessons learned from operational and administrative colleagues in the organization. Supports development of a comprehensive, targeted, highly useful knowledge base that allows staff throughout the organization to access mission-critical knowledge.

Responsibilities

» Captures the experiential knowledge of colleagues and experts throughout the organization as well as external stakeholders to populate and grow the organization's repository of valuable and sharable knowledge assets

» Continuously scans the organization for knowledge that is important for the organization's operations

» Interviews internal and external stakeholders to extract mission-critical experiences and lessons learned for further scaling up and sharing

» Manages the logistics, set-up, design, and implementation of synchronous knowledge-capturing activities, including meetings, focus groups, and workshops

» Designs and manages online capturing activities, including surveys, wikis, blogs, e-discussions

» Evaluates the usefulness of knowledge to be captured for replication and scale up

» Edits the knowledge assets in regards to language, formatting, and content

» Analyzes, synthesizes, and summarizes the captured knowledge and transforms it into formatted knowledge assets that are of high quality, standardized, and shareable

» Uses audiovisual tools to capture knowledge at high quality

» Populates the attributes and qualifiers of knowledge assets to ensure good findability

» Develops trusted relationships with a variety of stakeholders within and outside the organization

Qualifications

- » An advanced degree in journalism, English, knowledge management, or a related field and at least five years' applied experience in journalism

- » Excellent interview skills to ensure optimal documentation and extraction of knowledge derived from personal experiences

- » Excellent journalistic skills

- » Objectivity to identify and collect experiences that are deemed worth sharing

- » Profound interest and curiosity in the processes that make up the professional activities in the organization

- » Sound understanding of the professional environment and activities of the organization as well as of skills and competencies required to carry out the technical function within the organization

- » Motivation to share knowledge, successful practices, and lessons learned and interest in improving the effectiveness of the organization

- » Altruistic attitude and willingness to share knowledge

- » Sound time-management skills to adequately balance operational and knowledge work

- » Ability to objectively assess and analyze the skills, competencies, and expertise of co-workers

- » Ability and self-discipline to systematically reflect on past assignments to continuously improve

- » Ability to apply capturing activities such as interviews, observations, and group discussions

- » Writing and media production skills to process captured experiences in a way that they can be communicated or disseminated. This may include basic media and digital literacy skills

- » Ability to digest information and analyze, synthesize, and summarize it in clear and concise ways

- » Listening and observing skills to pick up events, facts, behaviors, and activities

- » Ability to ask relevant questions

- » Good interpersonal communication skills to relate with a variety of stakeholders, including senior colleagues

- » Emotional capacity and empathy to connect with others and to build trust

- » Typing and note-taking skills

- » Good facilitation skills to be able to tease out knowledge and information from other people

- » Familiarity with IT tools for producing knowledge materials

B.6 Audiovisual media specialist

Job description

The Audiovisual Media Specialist supports the capturing and recording of experiences and lessons learned throughout and beyond the organization. The specialist manages all technical logistics, including for location set-up, audio, lighting, and audiovisual (AV) equipment to ensure a smooth recording process. The specialist also supports the development of AV-based learning offerings and ensures knowledge assets and products are professionally edited.

Responsibilities

» Records interviews and other knowledge extraction activities using AV equipment

» Professionally edits AV recordings for further use in knowledge assets and more comprehensive knowledge and learning products

» Supports the knowledge-capturing specialist with all technology-based tools and processes

» Helps locate and maintain a technically suitable environment in which the recording will take place

Qualifications

» A bachelor's degree in audiovisual media, multimedia design, videography, or a related field and at least five years' applied experience as a cameraman and/or video editor

» Excellent understanding of AV equipment and recording options available to ensure good quality knowledge capturing

» Excellent audio and video editing skills with a good grasp of AV editing technologies and tools

» Good communication skills

» Good interpersonal skills a plus

B.7 Instructional/Learning designer

Job description

The Instructional/Learning Designer is in charge of curriculum development for the learning offerings of the organization. The designer is responsible for ensuring that both classroom-based and distance learning offerings yield the maximum learning results for the audiences, using a range of learning methods, tools, and technologies. The designer closely collaborates with subject matter experts and transforms technical content into high-impact learning experiences.

Responsibilities

» Communicate effectively in visual, oral, and written form

» Apply current instructional-design research and theory to create engaging learning experiences

» Conduct learning needs assessments to understand the skills gaps of the target audiences

» Design comprehensive learning curriculums or programs

» Select and use a variety of instructional design techniques for determining the most effective learning modalities, methods, and tools to ensure maximum learning impact

» Develop a sound understanding of the audiences, and design learning offerings based on specific learning objectives

» Develop a good understanding of the specific constraints of the audience, including location, availability, and language skills

» Continuously scan the market for existing and emerging technologies for use in an instructional environment, including state-of-the-art tools and techniques

» Select, modify, or create a learning-design model appropriate for a given learning offering

» Use a variety of instructional-design techniques to define and sequence the instructional content and related interactive activities

» Design learning offerings that reflect a deep understanding of the diversity of learning styles

» Evaluate and assess the impact of the organization's learning offerings

» Plan and manage projects for the development of learning offerings

» Implement and use the organization's learning management system to administrate and organize learning offerings

Qualifications

» An advanced degree in instructional/learning design, knowledge management, or a related field and at least five years' applied experience in designing learning offerings for face-to-face, distance, and blended delivery modalities

» Practical experience in developing classroom-based learning and e-learning offerings

» Ability to base learning offerings on the content of the organization's operations

» Ability to create innovative, interactive, and engaging content to increase learning impact

» Well-versed in the use of training and multimedia authoring tools

» Familiarity with various learning management systems

» Sound knowledge of common standards such as SCORM

» Ability to design agendas for learning events and activities that build on modern learning theory and include a high degree of interaction and reflection

» Well versed in the techniques of assessing the effectiveness of learning offerings

» Good technical writing skills

» Natural curiosity about instructional/learning design and about the mission of the organization

C.   Knowledge Capturing

C.1   Example: Knowledge asset prepared by the Federal Ministry of Agriculture and Rural Development (FMARD), Nigeria

FEDERAL MINISTRY OF AGRICULTURE
AND RURAL DEVELOPMENT

Department:
Farm Input Support Services (FISS)

Geopolitical Zone/State:
North Central/Niger State, Nigeria

Target Audience: Farmers, Agro Dealers, Extension Workers

Keywords: fertilizer, adulterated fertilizer, inorganic fertilizer, adulteration, identification, quick detection, smallholder farmer, purchase fertilizer, buying fertilizer

Author(s) and Contact Information:
L.C. Akudinobi (FISS) loveakus@ yahoo.com; Michael Ameh (FDA) michaelameh83@gmail.com; Bright Onyenze (P&PC) onyenzebright@ yahoo.com; Bethel Ohanenye (FDA) bethel4joshe@yahoo. com; Ajakaiye Haruna (HRM) harunadewale@gmail.com; Mathew Omirigbe (FDA) ommirigbem@ yahoo.com; O.G. Ajani (VPCS) ajanitimothy99@gmail.com

How Farmers Can Identify Adulterated Inorganic Fertilizers

Executive summary

Fertilizer is one of the basic inputs needed for increased agricultural productivity in Nigeria. Over the years, the Nigerian government has been promoting the complementary use of both inorganic and organic fertilizers to ensure increased agricultural productivity, which will result in sustained food security of the country.

One of the greatest challenges facing increased agricultural productivity in the rural area is adulterated fertilizer. The reason is that some smallholder farmers lack the knowledge about how to identify adulterated inorganic fertilizer, which could come in the form of bagging, wrong labeling, misbranding, and underweight bags.

This document provides lessons learned from a progressive farmer, Ahaji Abubakir, located in Chaza Village in Suleja Local Government Area in Niger State, combined with information from interviews with Mrs. L.C. Akudinobi, Deputy Director of Farm Input Supply Services. It presents the action taken by the farmer and good practices in evaluating fertilizer packages to ensure that he uses good quality fertilizer in his farming operations in order to get the maximum yield of crops from his 2 hectare farm.

The process of quick identification of adulterated inorganic fertilizer is highly recommended for our farmers to succeed in their farming business. It is also recommended that both the agro dealers and the farmers be educated and well trained on quality control issues for easy identification of adulterated fertilizer thereby checking the sale of adulterated fertilizer in the country.

Context and challenge

The Nigerian government has been promoting the use of inorganic fertilizer to ensure increased agricultural productivity, which will in turn result in sustained food security of the country. The government provides a subsidy through the Growth Enhancement Scheme (GES) to incentivize its use. Nigeria agricultural production is characterized by the involvement of small-scale farmers whose farm holdings range between 0.5 to 3 hectares of land. Most food consumed in the country is produced by this category of farmers.

The small-scale farmers complained of poor yield even after the application of fertilizer. This problem occurred mostly in farms owned by small-scale farmers. A farmer named Alhaji Abubakir from Chaza village in Suleja Local Government Area of Niger State also experienced a low yield of crops. He was told that the use of inorganic fertilizer would increase crop performance while continuously cultivating on the same piece of land. The expected high productivity could be sustained on the proper use of fertilizer. On the use of inorganic fertilizer, the expected increase in crop performance was not realized.

Before 1996, the sale of fertilizer was the sole responsibility of the various arms of the government i.e., federal, state, and local governments, hence the quality of fertilizers was assured. With the liberalization of the fertilizer subsector, the private sector was involved in the importation, blending, and sale of fertilizers. Some of the people involved in adulteration and sale of adulterated fertilizers include some middlemen in the distribution chain, agro-dealers, blenders, and importers.

The glaring low yield of crops was noticed mostly in the wet season when the demand for the commodity was highest. This may be attributed to the use of adulterated (poor quality) fertilizer among other reasons.

Adulteration is the act of selling debased materials (fertilizer with foreign mixture) for the purposes of making huge/quick profit. These include:

» Nonfertilizer material mixed with fertilizer

» Nonfertilizer materials misbranded and sold as fertilizer materials and as high-analysis fertilizer

» Misbranding of fake fertilizer materials as high-analysis fertilizer

» Cheaper fertilizer misbranded and sold as costly fertilizer

» Cheaper fertilizer mixed with costly fertilizer

» Misbranding or adulteration of low-grade fertilizer as high-analysis fertilizer

Application of adulterated fertilizer results in poor yield of crops. Soil structure and underground water are also negatively impacted.

Some of the common adulterants found in the Nigerian fertilizer markets are as follows:

Name of fertilizer	Common Adulterants
Urea	Common Salt, White River Sand
Di Ammonium Sulphate (DAP)	Clay, Rock Phosphate, Limestone
Single Superphosphate (SSP)	Clay, Gypsum
Muriate of Potash (MOP)	Sand, Red Earth
NPK Complexes	SSP, Rock Phosphate, NPK mixtures

The main challenge faced by Alhaji Abubakir was lack of or limited knowledge on how to quickly identify adulterated inorganic fertilizer before its purchase from the agro-dealers. Most rural farmers had not been trained on quick detection of adulterated fertilizers.

Adulteration of fertilizer was caused by the desire of some unscrupulous agro-dealers to make quick and enormous gains. Furthermore, scarcity and insufficient access to fertilizer during peak demand periods of fertilizer use, high cost of fertilizer, and cash constraint are among the major reasons that encourage the sale of adulterated fertilizer.

The consequences of the use of adulterated fertilizer include low crop and soil productivity, and probable pollution of ground water.

Action steps and solutions

Through experience over a period of time, Alhaji Abubakir learned how to identify adulterated fertilizer by looking for problems in these four areas:

- » Bagging and bagging materials
- » Labeling
- » Branding
- » Short-weight bags

He used the following methods to identify adulterated fertilizer. **Brand of fertilizer:** Ensure that the fertilizer brand is specified on the bag. **Labels on the bag:** Ensure that the labels on the bags are clearly written showing nutrient content, type of fertilizer, expiry date, company name, logo, etc.

Well labeled and branded Fertilizer showing company name, email, type of fertilizer, nutrient content, etc

Well labeled and branded bag showing the logo, company, type of fertilizer, nutrient content, batch number, etc.

Well labeled and branded bFertilizer showing the company name, logo, type of fertilizer, etc.

Request the agro-dealer to provide a weighing balance. If the fertilizer bag does not weigh up to the guaranteed weight, then it is adulterated.

Cellophane

Granular integrity

Good quality NPK
20-10-10 with cellophane
inner linning and good
granular integrity

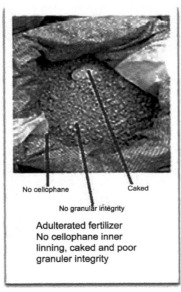

No cellophane

Caked

No granular integrity

Adulterated fertilizer
No cellophane inner
linning, caked and poor
granuler integrity

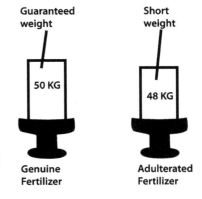

Ensure that fertilizer bag has an **inner lining** made of cellophane. This ensures that moisture is not absorbed from the atmosphere. Volatile nutrients are also conserved and are not lost to the atmosphere.

Outer bagging material of high quality cannot easily break. Dropping the bag from a height of about 2 meters is used to identify the quality of the bagging material. If it did not break on dropping from that height, then it is a good quality bag.

Granular integrity: The granules should be strong so as not to easily break into powder during hand feeling, not caked, should not be moist or powdery, etc.

Buy fertilizer from an agro-dealer that registered with the Federal/State Government and sells genuine fertilizers is advised.

Alhai Abubakir also trained farmers close to him on how to identify adulterated inorganic fertilizers, where to source the fertilizers, why they should avoid buying unwholesome fertilizers and the appropriate authority to report agro-dealers that sell adulterated fertilizer.

Results

By taking the above measures, Alhaji Abubakir reaped the benefits of his investment in fertilizer application in terms of commensurate increase in the yield of crops.

He was able to identify adulterated fertilizer by examining the bags and determining the weight of the bag using the weighing balance thereby ensuring that he is not cheated. He was able to make informed choices on brands and grades of fertilizer to buy crop specific and soil specific fertilizers.

Alhaji Abubakir continuously cultivates yam, maize and guinea corn on the same piece of land. He is called a successful farmer because there was increased productivity in his farm as a result of the use of good quality fertilizer in his farming operations. He has been using the income from the sales of the excess proceeds from his farm to marry more wives and send his children to school or to learn crafts.

Lessons learned

Alhaji Abubakir's experience clearly indicates that a small-scale farmer can easily identify adulterated fertilizer by observing the fertilizer bag. However, farmers need not go through trial and error as he did, in learning how to avoid adulterated fertilizer. Through sharing his lessons learned and experiential knowledge, Alhaji Abubakir was able to help other farmers improve their own productivity and contribute to the well-being of the community. Sharing this information will help to avoid costly lessons of experience and frustration of crop productivity.

Recommendations

Alhaji Abubakir recommends that small-scale farmers should always observe the bag, label, brand and the weight of the fertilizer to quickly identify an adulterated product.

He also suggested that problems like this would be avoided in the future by training and re-training both farmers and agro-dealers on identification of adulterated inorganic fertilizer.

Resources and reference materials

- » Mrs. L.C. Akudinobi, Deputy Director, Farm Input Support Services, FMARD
- » Alhaji Abubakir, Chaza Village in Suleja Local Government Area in Niger State
- » Fertilizer manuals for Extension agents
- » International fertilizer Development Centre Website
- » Fertilizer Analysis Manual
- » Introduction to Crop production
- » Fertilizer Use and Management Practices for Crops in Nigeria

D.   Knowledge-Sharing Tools and Templates

1.   Overview: Knowledge-Sharing Instruments and Activities

2.   Knowledge-Sharing Activity:

   a.   Planning Questionnaire

   b.   Implementation Checklist

   c.   Evaluation Form

   d.   Follow-Up Questionnaire

3.   Template for After-Action Review Report

D.1   Overview: Knowledge-sharing instruments and activities

As defined in the World Bank's (2015) guide *The Art of Knowledge Exchange*, instruments are the vehicles for knowledge sharing as they move the participants closer to realizing their change objectives. Their strength is fueled by knowledge-sharing activities, which form the building blocks of instruments. Instruments can be used alone or in combination to form a knowledge-sharing program. Similarly, instruments can consist of one or many activities combined. The guide provides detailed descriptions of each instrument and activity.

Instruments	Activities	
1. Short-term engagements	**1. Presentation**	**4. Analytical**
• Conference	• Demonstration	• After-action review
• Expert visit	• Expert panel	• Focus group
• Knowledge fair	• Lightning talks	• Interview
• Study tour	• Poster session	• Self-assessment
• Workshop	• Report	• Survey
2. Medium-term engagements	• Storytelling	• SWOT analysis
• Competition/challenge	**2. Discussion**	
• Knowledge jam	• Anecdote circle	
• Multistakeholder dialogue/consultation	• Brainstorming	
3. Long-term engagements	• Buzz session	
• Community of practice	• E-discussion	
• Twinning	• Knowledge café	
	• Peer assist	
	3. Experimental	
	• Action planning	
	• Book sprint	
	• Field visit	
	• Fishbowl	
	• Role play	
	• Secondment	
	• Simulation	

D.2.a   Knowledge-sharing activity: Planning questionnaire

1. Name of Organization: _____

2. URL: _____

3. Location:

   a. City: _____

   b. State: _____

   c. Country: _____

4. Please attach an organizational profile or use the space below to provide us with relevant background for your organization. This information will help us understand better your own context as we design our knowledge exchange.

5. What are the challenges you face?

6. Please type in the space below 5-10 specific questions that you have for us.

7. How do you intend to implement what you learned?

8. Duration of the exchange: _____ (days)

9. Please indicate in the space below your preferred time (week, month, year) for the exchange:

10. Check the boxes to indicate the type of participants involved in the exchange. In addition, please indicate the number of participants next to the ones you selected:

    ☐ Policy makers   _____ persons

    ☐ Senior management   _____ persons

    ☐ Middle management   _____ persons

    ☐ Technical specialists   _____ persons

    ☐ Faculty/Students   _____ persons

    ☐ Other (please explain below) _____ persons

11. Members of the delegation proficient in English? _____ persons

12. What do you think we can learn from you?

Your Contact Information

Surname: _____

First Name: _____

Position in the Organization: _____

E-mail: _____

Mailing Address: _____

D.2.b   Knowledge-sharing activity: Implementation checklist

Knowledge-Sharing Activity Implementation	Done: yes/no
PARTICIPANTS	
• All relevant participants, change agents, and decision makers identified	
• All invitations prepared, signed, and sent out	
• Participants' knowledge needs clarified	
LOGISTICS	
• All visa arrangements supported (special invitation letters)	
• International and local travel arrangements for participants made (airport pick-up, transfers to different venues, etc.)	
• Accommodations booked and meals organized, including special meal requests	
• All financial arrangements clarified and confirmed (allowances, etc.)	
• All venues, seating arrangements, and additional equipment (flip charts, markers, etc.) confirmed	
• Technology arrangements made (projector, audio equipment, etc.)	
• Interpretation arrangements made (simultaneous interpretation team, interpretation booth, and audio equipment)	
• Room decorations prepared	
• Name tags printed and finalized	
• Recording and capturing arrangements made (video recording, interviews with participants, etc.)	
• Precautions taken for potential challenges (adverse weather, late arrivals, etc.)	
• Additional tours organized (field visits, culture program, etc.)	
CONTENT	
• Learning objectives and goals clarified with participants	
• Agenda, sessions, and activities prepared and finalized	
• Speakers and resource persons identified, invited, and confirmed	
• All presentations and supporting media prepared and tested for delivery	
• All relevant support documents prepared and printed	
• Registration and evaluation forms developed and printed	
TEAM	
• Organizing team assembled	
• Senior management informed and invited	
• Facilitation team identified, confirmed, and briefed	
• Rapporteurs identified, confirmed, and briefed	
• Administrative support team identified, confirmed, and briefed	

D.2.c Knowledge-sharing activity: Evaluation form

Please complete the following questions to help us improve our future knowledge exchanges.

1. How would you rate the following factors:

	1 = Very Low	2	3	4	5 = Very High
The overall quality of the knowledge exchange					
The overall usefulness of the knowledge exchange					
The degree to which the knowledge exchange achieved the intended objectives					
The quality of the resources provided to you during the exchange					

2. Was the time allocated to each of the sessions adequate?

   ☐ Yes

   ☐ No (Please indicate which session needed more time:)

3. What worked best during the exchange?

4. What would you recommend to improve the exchange?

5. What are the key messages you are taking away from the knowledge exchange?

6. How will you apply the knowledge gained from the exchange in your organization?

D.2.d   Knowledge-sharing activity: Follow-up questionnaire

1. What, if anything, has changed in your work or for your organizations as a result of the knowledge exchange?

2. What challenges have you faced in your own context in implementing what you have learned during the knowledge exchange?

3. What has been the most beneficial aspect of the knowledge exchange for your work or your organization?

4. Looking back, are there any aspects of the knowledge exchange that you now feel should have been handled differently?

5. What barriers did you encounter since the knowledge exchange took place? Would you need additional assistance to overcome them?

6. Do you have additional comments and suggestions for further learning from practical experiences?

D.3   Template for after-action review report

Team/Project Name: _____

Project/Event Reviewed:

Date of Review: _____

When this review was completed:

☐ During project
☐ After project completion

Participants

Name	Job Title	Role in Team

Project/Event Summary:

What went well and why?

(What were the successful steps taken toward achieving your objective?)

Success	How to Ensure Future Success

What can be improved and how?

(What could have been done better? What can we do differently in similar situations in the future to ensure success? What would be your advice to future project teams?)

What Can Be Improved?	Recommendations

GLOSSARY

Italicized terms have their own entry.

Action learning

A "dynamic process that involves a small group of people solving real problems, while at the same time focusing on what they are learning and how their learning can benefit each group member, the group itself, and the organization as a whole" (Marquardt and Berger 2014, 181; see also Marquardt 2004). For individuals, action learning can create insights that can improve self-confidence. It can improve our ability to better reflect on our actions. At the team level, action learning fosters communication and collaboration. At the organizational level, it is a great way to increase knowledge flows across hierarchies and organizational boundaries (Schwandt and Marquardt 1999).

Blended learning

A formal education program in which a student learns at least in part through online delivery of content and instruction while still attending a "brick and mortar" school, with some element of student control over time, place, path, or pace. Face-to-face classroom methods are combined with computer-mediated activities.

Content management system (CMS)

Computer application that allows publishing, editing, and modifying content, as well as organizing, deleting, and maintenance, from a central interface. Such systems provide procedures to manage workflow in a collaborative environment. CMSs are often used to run websites containing blogs and news. Many corporate and marketing websites use CMSs, which typically avoid the need for hand coding.

Cross-functional team

A team whose members come from different organizational functions or have different specialties working together to accomplish a task. Usually cross-functional teams consist of individuals working at the same level of hierarchy in an organization.

Decision support system (DSS)

A computer-based information system that serves the management, operations, and planning levels of an organization (usually at middle and higher management levels). It aids decision making in a rapidly changing environment (unstructured and semistructured decision problems) by compiling useful information from a combination of raw data, documents, and personal knowledge. DSSs can be either fully computerized, human, or a combination of both. While academics have perceived

DSSs as a tool to support decision-making process, DSS users see it as a tool to facilitate organizational processes.

Distance learning

A mode of delivering education and instruction, often on an individual basis, to students who are not physically present in a traditional setting such as a classroom. Distance education courses that require a physical on-site presence for any reason (including taking examinations) have been referred to as *blended learning*.

E-learning

The use of information and communication technologies (ICT) in education. E-learning includes numerous types of media delivered via TV, CD-ROM, intranet/extranet, and other web-based learning. E-learning is usually supported by local or web-based network access. It can occur in or out of the classroom as asynchronous learning (individuals accessing material at separate times) or as instructor-led, synchronous learning. E-learning is suited to *distance learning* and flexible learning because it can be self-paced, but it can also be used in conjunction with face-to-face teaching, in which case the term *blended learning* is commonly used.

Experiential (or implicit) knowledge

Knowledge that resides in people's heads as intangible knowledge but which can be converted into *explicit knowledge* through a process of documentation and capturing.

Explicit (or codified) knowledge

Knowledge that has been articulated, codified, stored, and readily transmitted to others. The information contained in textbooks, manuals, documents, procedures, case studies, and how-to videos are examples of explicit knowledge. Polanyi (1966) defines explicit or codified knowledge as "knowledge that can be transmitted by formal systematic language" (cited in Schwandt and Marquardt 1999, 127). In Zack (1999, 46), "explicit knowledge is more precisely and formally articulated, although removed from the original context of creation or use (e.g. an abstract mathematical formula derived from physical experiments)."

Extrinsic motivation

The "tendency to perform activities for known external rewards, whether they be tangible (e.g. money) or psychological (e.g. praise)" (Brown 2007, 143). Extrinsic rewards can include recognition, honors, pay raises, bonuses, *training*, and career development.

Force-field theory

A theory that organizations are subject to forces that simultaneously pull toward change and resist it. Force-field analysis provides a framework for looking at the helping and hindering forces that are influencing the current situation (Swanson and Creed 2013).

Formal organization structure

The functions, hierarchies, reporting relationships, and rules of an organization.

Intrinsic motivation

Behavior based on intangible rewards that arise from an individual's own personal values and motivations. They can include a sense of accomplishment, pride and satisfaction derived from the completing a challenging task, and the pursuit of learning. They are not necessarily tied to achieving a specific objective. Citing Malone and Lepper (1987), Tran (2014, 178) notes that an activity is described as intrinsically motivating if "people engage in it for its own sake rather than in order to receive some external reward or avoid some punishment. We use the words fun, interesting, captivating, enjoyable, and intrinsically motivating all more or less interchangeably to describe such activities."

Knowledge asset

A digital document or collection of media containing knowledge about a specific question or challenge. Typically short and learner-oriented, a knowledge asset presents key lessons learned from an operational experience and provides decision-making support for one particular challenge. The story it presents follows a standardized format—tracing the problem, actions, results, lessons, and recommendations—that makes the asset a self-contained lesson. It should be validated in a peer-review process and formatted with metadata allowing it to be found within a larger *knowledge repository*. The model of a knowledge asset is also used in the concept of mental "theories of action," which describes behavior at individual, group, and organizational levels. Similar to the structure of a knowledge asset, a simple theory of action would include a basic description of the context, the problem to be addressed (goal), and a strategy to take action to overcome the problem, assuming conditions are comparable (Argyris and Schön 1974 and 1978).

Knowledge capturing

The process of converting the knowledge or experience that resides in the mind of an individual into an explicit representation, whether in print, electronic, or multimedia form.

Knowledge-capturing team

A team that systematically and uniformly documents lessons learned from operational experiences that have not yet been explicitly recorded or are difficult to record. Its goal is to capture critical insights and takeaways for potential replication elsewhere. Team members possess an ability to quickly grasp the key challenges and solution paths in a journalistic way. Their most common techniques are interviews and focus groups.

Knowledge-creating organization

An organization that is able to translate *tacit knowledge* into *explicit knowledge* applicable to a different context and formalize it. Over time, the new knowledge itself becomes tacit and available to become explicit in yet another context (Nonaka and Takeuchi 1995). To achieve these transformations, managers and staff need to engage in continuous reflection at the individual, team, and organizational levels, and time and space for such reflection needs to be provided.

Knowledge exchange

See *Knowledge sharing*.

Knowledge hub

An institution or network dedicated to capturing, sharing, and exchanging development experiences with national and international partners to accelerate development (Government of Indonesia and others 2012).

Knowledge management

A discipline promoting an integrated approach to identifying, capturing, evaluating, retrieving, and sharing all of an enterprise's information assets. As defined by the Gartner Group (Duhon 1998), these assets may include databases, documents, policies, procedures, and previously uncaptured expertise and experience in individual workers. It is intended to improve efficiency and the quality of products and services and to achieve innovations. Although knowledge management overlaps with *organizational learning*, the former may be distinguished by a greater focus on knowledge as a strategic asset and on encouraging *knowledge sharing*. Knowledge management is an enabler of organizational learning.

Knowledge repository

A data storage system that can comprise multiple, networked technologies. It allows for centralized management of, and provision of access to, *knowledge assets* and supports resource management to add, maintain, update, recycle, and discard knowledge assets. Knowledge repositories are also referred to as *knowledge-management* or knowledge-resource platforms.

Knowledge sharing

A subset of *knowledge management* encompassing the exchange of knowledge (information, skills, experiences, or expertise) within and across organizations. Although it can be one-directional, knowledge sharing in most cases is a two-way or multilateral exchange in which the parties learn from each other. Knowledge sharing is more than mere communication because much knowledge in organizations is hard to articulate. In development work, some knowledge sharing has a regional aspect. For example, South-South knowledge sharing refers to exchanges among partners and peers across developing countries.

Learning management system (LMS)

A software application for the administration, documentation, tracking, reporting, and delivery of *e-learning* education courses or *training* programs. LMSs range from systems for managing training and educational records to software for distributing online or *blended learning* courses over the Internet with features for online collaboration. Colleges and universities use LMSs to deliver online courses and augment on-campus courses. Corporate training departments use LMSs to deliver online training as well as to automate record-keeping and employee registration.

Learning organization

"An organization that is skilled at creating, acquiring, and transferring knowledge and at modifying behavior to reflect new knowledge and insights" (DuBrin 2005, 410). Learning organizations exhibit five main characteristics: personal mastery, mental models, a shared vision, team learning, and—the fifth element that integrates them—systems thinking (Senge 2006).

Organizational behavior

The study of individual and team behavior in an organization, of the interaction between individuals and the organization, and of the organization itself.

Organizational culture

According to DuBrin (2005, 337–39), "a system of shared values and beliefs that influence worker behavior.... Often its origin lies in the values, administrative practices, and personality of the founder or founders. Also the leader's vision can have a heavy impact on culture.... Organizational culture responds to and mirrors the conscious and unconscious choices, behavior patterns, and prejudices of top-level managers." DuBrin 2005 posits nine dimensions of organizational culture: values, organizational stories with underlying meanings, myths, degree of stability, resource allocations and rewards, rites and rituals, sense of ownership, belief in a higher purpose, and innovativeness.

Organizational effectiveness

The extent to which an organization delivers on its mandate and fulfills the demand of stakeholders it engages with.

Organizational learning

An area of knowledge within organizational theory that studies the way an organization learns and adapts. It is also defined as "a system of actions, actors, symbols, and processes that enables an organization to transform information into valued knowledge, which in turn increases its long-run adaptive capacity" (Schwandt and Marquardt 1999, 43). "Organizational Learning involves making tacit theories of action explicit so that people can become aware of, critically examine, and change them.... it facilitates accountability by increasing self-awareness and enhancing the ability to exercise conscious choice and intention" (Lipshitz, Friedman, and Popper 2007, 122). To increase the organization's readiness one must develop the capability to learn how to learn. Policy, structures, and skills are needed to do so (Schön 1975).

Organizational memory

Shared interpretations of an organization's past as related by the members of the organization. Organizational memory can be "episodic" or "semantic." The former describes memories of a person who had the experiences contained in the memories, whereas the latter is independent of those experiences—for example, through retelling of stories by someone who was not part of an actual experience (Schwandt and Marquardt 1999, 206).

Tacit knowledge

The knowledge in people's heads. Tacit knowledge is personal, context-specific, and therefore hard to formalize and communicate (Schwandt and Marquardt 1999, 206). Tacit knowledge is subconsciously understood and applied; difficult to articulate; developed from direct experience and action; and usually shared through highly interactive conversation, storytelling, and shared experience.

Training

The acquisition of knowledge, skills, and competencies intended to improve one's capabilities, productivity, and performance. It forms the core of apprenticeships while also being increasingly used for professional development—to upgrade and update skills throughout one's working life.

Value

The importance an individual or group attaches to something that serves as a guide to action.

REFERENCES

ADB (Asian Development Bank). 2011. *Guidelines for Knowledge Partnerships*. Manila.

APQC (American Productivity and Quality Center). 2003. *Measuring the Impact of Knowledge Management*. Houston.

———. 2009. "Using Investment to Ensure ROI on KM Efforts." ftp://public.dhe.ibm.com/services/us/gbs/bus/hcm/rbtt/kmroi.pdf.

———. 2013. *Transferring and Applying Critical Knowledge (Best Practices Report)*. Houston. www.apqc.org/knowledge-base/documents/ transferring-and-applying-critical-knowledge-best-practices-report.

Argyris, Chris, and Donald Schön. 1974. *Theory in Practice: Increasing Professional Effectiveness*. San Francisco: Jossey-Bass.

———. 1978. *Organizational Learning: A Theory of Action Perspective*. Reading, MA: Addison-Wesley.

Bhatt, Dilip. 2000. "EFQM [European Foundation for Quality Management]: Excellence Model and Knowledge Management Implications." 2000. www.comp.dit.ie/dgordon/Courses/ResearchMethods/Countdown/3Elements.pdf.

Brown, Lois V., ed. 2007. *Psychology of Motivation*. New York: Nova Science Publishers.

Craig, Robert L. 1996. *The ASTD Training and Development Handbook: A Guide to Human Resource Development*. New York: McGraw-Hill.

Crossan, Mary M., Henry W. Lane, and Roderick E. White. 1999. "An Organizational Learning Framework: From Intuition to Institution." *Academy of Management Review* 24 (3): 522–37.

Davenport, Thomas H., and Laurence Prusak. 1998. *Working Knowledge: How Organizations Manage What They Know*. Boston: Harvard Business School Press.

Drucker, Peter F. 1993. "The Rise of the Knowledge Society." *Wilson Quarterly* 17 (2): 52–71.

DuBrin, Andrew J. 2005. *Fundamentals of Organizational Behavior*. 3rd edition. Cincinnati, OH: South-Western College Publishing.

Duhon, Bryant. 1998. "It's All in Our Heads." *Inform* 12 (8): 8–13.

Gawande, Atul. 2009. *The Checklist Manifesto: How to Get Things Right*. New York: Henry Holt.

Gino, Francesca, and Bradley Staats. 2015. "Why Organizations Don't Learn." *Harvard Business Review* (November): 110–18.

Government of Indonesia, Japan International Cooperation Agency, UN Development Programme, and the World Bank. 2012. Bali Communiqué by the Co-Organizers, High-Level Meeting "Towards Country-Led Knowledge Hubs." July 10. wbi.worldbank.org/sske/news/world-bank-support-knowledge-hubs.

IEG (Independent Evaluation Group). 2014. *Learning and Results in World Bank Operations: How the Bank Learns, Evaluation 1*. Washington, DC: World Bank.

———. 2015. *Learning and Results in World Bank Operations: Toward a New Learning Strategy, Evaluation 2*. Washington, DC: World Bank.

Kaplan, Robert S., and David P. Norton. 1996. "Using the Balanced Scorecard as a Strategic Management System." *Harvard Business Review* (January-February): 75–85.

Knowles, Malcolm S., Elwood F. Holton III, and Richard A. Swanson. 2012. *The Adult Learner: The Definitive Classic in Adult Education and Human Resource Development*, 7th edition. New York: Routledge.

Kolb, David A. 1984. *Experiential Learning: Experience as the Source of Learning and Development*. Englewood Cliffs, NJ: Prentice Hall.

Lipshitz, Raanan, Victor J. Friedman, and Micha Popper. 2007. *Demystifying Organizational Learning*. Thousand Oaks, CA: Sage Publications.

Malone, Thomas W., and Mark R. Lepper. 1987. "Making Learning Fun: A Taxonomy of Intrinsic Motivations for Learning." In *Aptitude, Learning, and Instruction, Vol. 3: Conative and Affective Process Analyses*, edited by Richard E. Snow and Marshall J. Farr, 223–53. Hillsdale, NJ: Lawrence Erlbaum Associates.

Marquardt, Michael J. 2004. "Action Learning: A Powerful New Training Tool for Developing Individuals, Teams and Organizations." *By George!* The George Washington University, February 18. www.gwu.edu/~bygeorge/021804/actionlearning.html.

Marquardt, Michael J., and Nancy O. Berger. 2014. *Global Leaders for the Twenty-First Century*. Albany, NY: State University of New York Press.

Nonaka, Ikujiro, and Hirotaka Takeuchi. 1995. *The Knowledge-Creating Company: How Japanese Companies Create the Dynamics of Innovation*. New York: Oxford University Press.

Polanyi, Michael. 1966. *The Tacit Dimension*. Garden City, NY: Doubleday. Chicago: University of Chicago Press, 2009, foreword by Amartya Sen.

Schön, Donald A. 1975. "Deutero-Learning in Organizations: Learning for Increased Effectiveness." *Organizational Dynamics* 4 (1): 2–16.

Schwandt, David R. 1994. "Organizational Learning as a Dynamic Sociological Construct: Theory and Research." In *Proceedings of the 12th International Conference of the System Dynamics Society* 2: 55-66. Albany, NY: System Dynamics Society. www.systemdynamics.org/conferences/1994/proceed/papers_vol_2/schwandt.pdf.

Schwandt, David R., and Michael J. Marquardt. 1999. *Organizational Learning: From World-Class Theories to Global Best Practices*. Boca Raton, FL: CRC Press.

Senge, Peter, M. 2006. *The Fifth Discipline: The Art and Practice of the Learning Organization*. Revised edition. New York: Crown Publishers.

Smith, Heather A., and James D. McKeen. 2003. "Instilling a Knowledge-Sharing Culture." Working paper, Queen's University School of Business, Kingston, Canada. wikis.uit.tufts.edu/confluence/download/attachments/54161086/Instilling a Knowledge-Sharing Culture.pdf.

Swanson, Donald James, and Andrew Shawn Creed. 2013. "Sharpening the Focus of Force Field Analysis." *Journal of Change Management* 14 (1): 28–47. doi:10.1080/14697017.2013.788052.

Tran, Ben. 2014. "Rhetoric of Play: Utilizing the Gamer Factor in Selecting and Training Employees." In *Psychology, Pedagogy, and Assessment in Serious Games,* edited by Thomas M. Connolly, Thomas Hainey, Elizabeth Boyle, Gavin Baxter, and Pablo Moreno-Ger, 175–203. Hershey, PA: IGI Global.

World Bank. 2015. *The Art of Knowledge Exchange*, 2nd edition. Washington, DC: World Bank. wbi.worldbank.org/sske/art-knowledge-exchange.

———. 2016. *Capturing Solutions for Learning and Scaling Up*. Washington, DC: World Bank.

Zack, Michael H. 1999. "Managing Codified Knowledge." *Sloan Management Review* 40 (4): 45–58.